ANGEL'S SHARE

AN AGENTS IRISH AND WHISKEY NOVEL

LAYLA REYNE

Angel's Share

Copyright © 2024 by Layla Reyne

Cover Design: Cate Ashwood; Cover Photography: Wander Aguiar; Cover Model: Matheus R.

Editing: Adam Mongaya; Proofreading: Lori Parks

First Edition

August, 2024

E-Book ISBN: 978-1-962010-10-8

Paperback ISBN: 978-1-962010-11-5

Content Warnings: Explicit sex; explicit language; violence; off-page death of a former spouse; off-page death of a parent; instances and/or discussion of homophobia and racism; use of a homophobic slur; and instances and/or discussion of depression and PTSD.

ABOUT THIS BOOK

FBI agent Aidan Talley just wanted to spend the holiday weekend cheering on his husband's basketball team. Instead, he's investigating a cargo theft for the family business and coming face-to-face with a loose end from the case that almost tore him and Jamie apart.

Coach Jameson Walker may spend his days on the sidelines now, but Jamie refuses to stay there when it comes to his husband. When Aidan is cornered by his past, Jamie will do whatever it takes to ground him in the present, including stepping back into his hacker shoes for the Bureau.

Aidan and Jamie thought they'd seen it all, but the City of Angels has more than one ghost in store for them. As revenge and redemption collide, Agents Irish and Whiskey will have to trust in their love and their partnership to solve the case for the family they have, for the one they lost, and for the one they want to call their own.

AUTHOR'S NOTE

It is with David-levels of embarrassment that I must admit the same-name genie has struck again. *Face palm* My affection for certain names cannot be kept in the bottle! For the avoidance of doubt, the Isabella in *Agents Irish & Whiskey* is not the same Isabella in *Fog City*. I blame this one on *Days of Our Lives*. Isabella was always my favorite. I have no such excuse for every Sean and Scotty.

Also, for the chronologically minded, this story is set in December 2023, several months after Marsh & Levi's re-wedding in *Best Play*. As a reminder, Aidan and Jamie first started working together in September 2016 and were married on March 17, 2018. And yes, Katie really is that old now. Yikes!

ONE

"Let's go, let's go, let's go!" On his feet, Aidan clapped and cheered as the players in red and blue raced down the court. Transition offense, executing the play he and his husband had practiced at the gym earlier that week. Only today, it wasn't him and Jamie jogging at their midlife best. Instead, the much younger, much faster guard who was coached by Jamie barreled down the lane, using his speed and size to get the basket and draw the foul.

"And one!" Danny shouted from the front row of their suite, pumping his fist and exchanging high fives with Levi and David beside him.

A row back, Aidan chuckled as he reached for his beer. The stout was local, not as good as his best friend's brew but better than expected, its thick texture and subtle spice befitting the holiday season. Less subtle were the purple and gold and silver and black decorations that festooned everything—the giant tree outside the arena, the digital scoreboards inside it, even the luxury box he'd rented out for their friends and family. Granted, he expected nothing less in Los Angeles. He flicked the purple ornament nestled in the garland at the end of his row. "Should have brought some orange and black decorations."

"*Or*," Mel said from Danny's other side, "they could've just waited to put all this shit up after this weekend."

"Hey!" Danny scoffed at his wife. "It's a *holiday* tourney, and it's *after* Thanksgiving. Fair game, chica."

"I don't care how early the holidays arrive," Lauren said from across the aisle. "As long as they show up with peppermint lattes." She flitted her fingers around her mug, her nails striped red and white and tipped in navy for Jamie's team. Beside her, Jax had dyed their mohawk the same, and their girlfriend, February, had woven red, white, and navy ribbons into her braided pigtails.

"Get in the hole!" Levi shouted, drawing Aidan's attention and his laughter. He'd gotten to know the San Diego ASAC over the last couple of years, and it was usually his husband, Marsh, the cyber agent on Aidan's left, who was the louder of the two—except when it came to basketball. Levi's alma mater had played in the first game of the tourney, and after a quick sweatshirt change, he and his son were cheering loudly beside Danny, gamely pulling for Jamie's team now.

On the sidelines, Jamie cheered for his players too, slapping their backs as the team's head coach called a huddle during the television timeout. As good as Jamie had been as an FBI agent, he was better at basketball and at coaching, a natural on the court in either capacity.

"He's really good at this," Marsh said, as if reading Aidan's mind. He tilted his beer bottle toward the court where Jamie had pulled aside a player, showing him something on a tablet. "With the kids too," Marsh added, before lowering his voice and asking, "You two ever think about having any?"

Aidan tipped back his bottle, savoring another sip as he gathered his thoughts and words, the matter . . . unresolved. He and Jamie still talked like it would happen one day, same as he and his late husband, Gabe, had done. Jamie was undeniably good with kids of all ages, they both liked them, and they both spent as much time with their niblings as they could, their favorite of whom, Katie, had just turned ten. And if that wasn't a punch to the I'm-old gut, Aidan didn't know what was. Time moved faster than any of them could keep up with. A blink and five years had gone by since he and Jamie were married. Five very busy years between Aidan's job as Special Agent in Charge of the FBI's San Francisco field office and Jamie's as an assistant coach for a D-I basketball program and occasional cyber consultant for the Bureau. Not to mention friends and family getting into trouble and falling into love, growing said family, as evidenced in this very suite. "We've talked about it, but making time . . ."

"I understand that," Marsh said with a laugh, and Aidan figured the cyber agent with temple grays under his cowboy hat did understand, better than most. "Always thought I would too, then twenty years in the military and trial by fire at the Bureau got in the way. Until . . ." His gaze slid a row ahead and the corners of his mouth tipped up as his husband and son argued over a call. "Sometimes they land in your lap when you least expect it."

"If I recall correctly, *you* landed in *their* lap."

"Same difference." Smiling wider, Marsh waggled his ring finger. "Happily ever after in the end." His fond gaze lingered another few seconds on Levi and David before returning to the game.

Same as Aidan's, even as his mind continued to wrestle with Marsh's innocent question. Or so it had seemed in that moment when Marsh asked. Unlike when his mom or sisters brought it up at family events, always out of Jamie's earshot. Aidan wondered if Jamie got the same questions from his mom and sister. Did he answer with the same "when the time is right" line as Aidan? What would he answer if Aidan asked? Should he ask? Aidan didn't feel a deep, hankering need for kids like he'd heard his sisters and his brothers-in-law talk about before they'd had theirs. For Aidan, it was more like an idle wondering that hummed low in his mind. But the time for idle wondering was dwindling, as was his stamina for diapers and all-nighters. If he and Jamie were to adopt, he'd lean more toward a child in need who was Katie's age or a little older, though the thought of raising a teen also sent a shiver racing up his spine.

A thunderous roar went up from the crowd, knocking Aidan out of the theoretical future and back into the here and now. Jamie's team was up with fifteen seconds left, and their best free throw shooter was at the line. He drained the first shot, making it a three-possession game.

"That should do it!" Marsh said, as Levi and David shouted "Victory!"

On the sidelines, Jamie was celebrating too, waving his arms and amping up the crowd, turning their box's direction and throwing them a stunning grin. The sheer joy on his face sent Aidan's heart racing, like five years hadn't passed at all. His joy, his love for the game was so infectious Aidan almost missed the shift in mood a row ahead.

"What happened?" Danny shouted over the crowd. He turned away from the crowd and hunched over, a hand over his other ear, trying to amplify the quiet. "They stole what?" His dark brows snapped together, distress clear in his pinched expression. "We'll be right there."

"What's going on?" Aidan asked, as Danny righted himself.

"Cargo theft at the port." As head of the family shipping empire, Danny would get that call, especially if the value of the stolen goods was significant. So would Mel, if she hadn't handed off chief of security duties a few months ago. Didn't mean she'd fully stepped away from the role.

"Off one of our ships?" she asked.

"Not exactly," Danny said, then waited for the final buzzer to sound and the cacophony of cheers to die down before continuing. "Goods were off-loaded from one of our ships onto a truck that was stolen from our yard."

"Contents?" Aidan asked.

"Can't tell you that, big bro. Not until it's official."

Aidan raised a brow. Danny was the last person to be a stickler for the rules. Which meant . . . "Real high value?" Danny nodded. "Angry buyer?" And nodded again. Artwork or jewels, if Aidan had to guess. Or cars, maybe. In any event, it would be official soon. "We've got a former colleague on the task force here in LA."

"And I'll call Matt," Marsh said, clearly having eavesdropped. "Levi and I would help too, but we're on a flight out to San Francisco tonight. If we don't make it, I'm gonna have an angry son and angrier niece to deal with."

"And I understand that," Aidan said. "Thanks for calling Matty in." He clasped Marsh's shoulder, then hustled for the stairs, weaving out of their box and down to the sideline, flashing the access badge Jamie always made sure he had for situations like this. "Jamie!" he shouted over the celebrating fans and players.

Jamie whipped around, his blue eyes wide and his grin big. "Did you see that drive?"

Aidan found it impossible not to return the smile, happy for his husband and the team, independent of the storm clouds brewing elsewhere. "That was the play we practiced earlier in the week."

"He nailed it!"

"Y'all did great tonight. Go celebrate with the team. I'll meet you back at the hotel later."

"You know you're always welcome," Jamie said, snagging his hand. "Everyone is!"

"I'd love to, but I'm headed to the port with Mel and Danny."

Jamie's smile dimmed, his fingers tightening around Aidan's. "What's going on?"

"Cargo theft." Aidan kept his own smile in place, unwilling to dampen this win for his husband. "Just want to be sure it gets into the right hands."

"Matty K?"

Aidan nodded, then flashed his free hand, fingers wide. "And Jazz Hands."

"Good call." Chuckling, Jamie pulled Aidan in for a quick but firm kiss. "Ring me if you need anything. And be careful."

"Always."

TWO

Aidan snaked his rented Outback through the Port of Long Beach, following Danny's and Mel's directions past the shipping terminal with its giant red cranes and through the seemingly endless container terminal, until they finally turned into the Talley Enterprises yard. "How do you keep all the ports straight?" he asked as he pulled in front of the modular office structure. "And where our yard is in each?"

"Muscle memory," Danny answered with a wink. "And generally making sure our yard is in the same directional quadrant at each port."

"You picked that up from Dad."

"I did!"

"There's also an app for that," Mel whispered conspiratorially, flashing her phone screen in his direction, before she followed Danny out of the car.

Aidan was glad to see the stress they'd both carried when leaving the arena had been somewhat eased by whatever texts and emails they'd been working through on the car ride over. Hopefully, the angry client was satisfied that they were giving the matter the attention it deserved, including Bureau assistance from Aidan and the other two agents waiting for them outside the office.

Aidan approached the black-haired agent first, arms open wide. "Happy holidays, Matty K!" He ignored the other agent's rolling dark eyes and yanked him into a hug. "We keep running into each other like this, and a certain ASAC we both know and love is gonna get jealous." Before landing in Southern California, Agent Matthew Kim had been partnered with Aidan's ASAC and Jamie's best friend, Cameron Byrne, when they'd both been assigned to Boston.

Agent Rick Lorton was no stranger either, previously reporting to Aidan in San Francisco. "Rick, it's been too long," Aidan said, hand outstretched to the field agent who used to moonlight as a cover model for romance novels to pay his Bay Area bills. Aidan didn't ask if his current salary was enough to cover LA rent; he wasn't Rick's boss any longer. "Wish it were under better circumstances. You both remember Mel and my brother Danny."

"What can you tell us?" Danny asked once the introductions were over.

"Truck driver had the cargo loaded," Rick said. "Left the truck running while he hopped out to take a leak in the office."

Danny wiped a hand down his face. "There are no less than a dozen 'Avoid Cargo Theft' signs on the way in here, and he does *that*?"

"Said there were plenty of people around," Matt replied. "Even some kids visiting the port on a school trip."

"Any of whom could be the thief," Mel said. "Video?"

"As soon as we can wrest it from LBPD."

"It's our video."

Rick held up a hand. "The detective on this case, Berat Namal, is former LAPD commercial crimes. Works for Long Beach now. He's severely overworked but well-versed in cargo theft. He's cooperated on all our cases together."

"He's also the only one still giving me the time of day on that jewel thief cold case," Matt said. "I'd like to stay in his good graces in case it ever gets hot again."

"Fair enough," Aidan said. "We don't mean to cause waves." Matt failed to stifle his laugh. "Got something to say, Matty K?"

"Not as long as you stop using that nickname."

Losing battle, and Matt knew it. Same as Aidan knew their attempt not to cause waves would likely fail too. But he really didn't want to on this case, for the sake of his brother and for the sake of the clearly exhausted man who trudged out of the office, his shoulders slumped and face drawn. Nevertheless, as Detective Namal glanced up and spied Rick and Matt, he flashed them a smile that was as nonhostile as any Aidan had ever seen from local law enforcement. "Rick, good to see you." Namal shook Rick's hand, then Matt's. "Agent Kim, good to see you too."

"Sorry to ruin your Friday," Matt said.

"Nah," he said with a wave of his hand. "You saved me from the holiday office party." Namal's gaze skipped past the known variables to the rest of their gathered group. "Gonna introduce me to your friends? You guys come straight from the tourney downtown?" Local, Aidan judged, by non-accent-California-accent, distinct enough from the San Francisco one to peg him as SoCal born and raised.

"Detective Berat Namal, this is my former boss," Rick said. "Special Agent in Charge Aidan Talley from the San

Francisco field office." He pointed at Aidan's game day sweatshirt. "His husband is an assistant coach for the team."

Namal pointed a different direction, toward the stacks of shipping containers just past the parking lot. "Talley? As in the name on the side of those? And on the boats?"

"The same," Aidan said with a nod. "Though he"—he jutted a thumb at Danny—"is the one in charge of the boats. My brother, Daniel Talley."

He shook Danny's hand, then aimed his sparkling hazel eyes at Mel. "And you, I suspect, are the one in charge of all of them."

"Melissa Cruz," Mel said, taking his offered hand. "Former SAC, former chief of security for Talley Enterprises. Filling in until the current chief gets here." She tilted her head toward Danny. "Also his wife."

"So I was right," he said, the warmth in his laughter reflected in his cheeks, color seeping back into the pale tan skin.

Aidan could see why Rick liked him. Smart, genial, and charming. Seemed Danny liked him too, chuckling and relaxing a measure further, deciding this was someone he could work with. "What do you need from us, detective?"

"Berat, please," he said. "We'll need manifests first and foremost, particularly what cargo was off-loaded and stolen so we know what we're looking for. Your captain and general counsel are stalling."

Aidan had heard those instructions in the car ride over, not that either of them needed to be told. The captain of the vessel was one of their most seasoned, and their general counsel also bore the last name Talley—Aidan's and Danny's older sister.

"It was headed across state lines," Mel said.

"Right," Berat replied. "So my jurisdiction to the gates," he said, gesturing the general direction of the exit, then at Matt and Rick. "Then yours. We'll all get a lot further if we work together, like we usually do."

"We're fine with that," Rick said before looking to Matt and Aidan, who each nodded.

"We'll get you those manifests," Danny said.

"*If* we can get the surveillance video," Aidan added.

Berat's victory smile fell. "Sure, but it won't show you anything. View was blocked by another vehicle when the thief climbed into the truck and drove off."

"Footage from the exit gates?" Mel asked. "Plates?"

"We've requested it. Port security is pulling it now." He leveled his gaze on Danny. "What was in that truck?"

"It's official now, baby bro," Aidan said. "Share with the class."

"The part that matters—red diamonds, multiple carats worth."

Matt's eyes grew wide. "That's at least multiple millions."

Danny nodded. "Plus various other luxury goods the owner was shipping into the country for his new home in Las Vegas. Insurance covered the lot up to twelve million."

Aidan whistled low. "You need to get that cargo back."

THREE

The electronic lock on the hotel room door engaged, and Jamie glanced first at the time on his laptop screen—eleven thirty—then at his husband, who was trying and failing to quietly sneak into the room.

"I'm still up."

Aidan lifted his chin, catching sight of him and exhaling a relieved sigh. "Are you watching tape?" he asked, a soft, sexy smirk curling up one corner of his mouth.

"Of course."

"I think you're supposed to enjoy the victory. At least a little." He removed his long-since-useful aviators from atop his head, tossed them and the contents of his pockets on the dresser, and toed off his shoes. Pitching his coat on the end of the bed, he ambled the rest of the way across the room to the corner couch and table where Jamie had posted up for the evening.

While rules required Jamie stay at the same hotel as the rest of the team, the reward points he and Aidan collectively accumulated usually ensured him an upgrade. And more space was never a bad thing when you were six-five, especially when your six-foot husband also joined you on the road. He closed his laptop and propped a foot against the table's pedestal, pushing the table back far enough for Aidan to slide in in front of him.

"If you're not partying," Aidan said as he raked a hand through his auburn hair, something Jamie would never tire of, "you should be sleeping."

Jamie snagged one of Aidan's hands and tugged him closer. Tugged him harder, forcing Aidan to climb onto the couch, his knees on either side of Jamie's hips, straddling his lap. Husband where he wanted him, Jamie looped his arms around Aidan's waist and brushed his lips over Aidan's. "I'll do both *after* we've won the tourney."

"Spoken like a true athlete." Aidan grinned, then snuck his tongue between Jamie's lips, deepening the kiss.

Something else Jamie would never tire of.

Leaning back into the corner, he drew Aidan down on top of him and slipped his hands under the hem of Aidan's sweatshirt, warming his December cool skin and lifting goose bumps in his wake. More than five years since they'd said *I do*, seven since they'd first been intimate, and they still had their moments of urgent need, when one sort of adrenaline or another—danger, victory, or lust—pushed them to desperation. But Jamie had come to appreciate these quiet, peaceful moments just as much. When they could exist in the same space together and fill it with soft touches and gentle kisses, reacquainting themselves after a long day, a trip out of town, or a trip to the corner store.

Not to say the quiet, peaceful moments didn't also stir

desire, the evidence hardening in Jamie's sweats. Behind Aidan's zipper too, his cock pressing against Jamie's hip. But Jamie didn't want to push for more without knowing exactly how long an evening Aidan had had. And if the evening was even over for him. Jamie had worked long enough for the Bureau to learn the unpredictable rhythms of the job. Yes, Aidan had emptied his pockets and taken off his shoes, but that didn't mean he wouldn't have to be out the door again soon.

Jamie drew back and rested his head on the top of the couch cushions. "Late night for you too," he said as he swept a wayward auburn strand off Aidan's forehead.

"Gonna be a later one for Danny."

"Case handled?"

"Jazz Hands is on it," Aidan said, complete with his fingers spread wide to make Jamie laugh. Rick had made one excited hand gesture when he'd thought his boss was gonna can his ass, and he'd been forever branded. "Matt too, and the local detective on the case seems cooperative."

"Want me to check him out?"

Aidan shook his head, then laid it on Jamie's shoulder. "I'm gonna trust Rick and Matt and let Daniel do his job. Above my pay grade."

Jamie laughed some more and ran his fingers through Aidan's hair, smiling at the silver and white strands peeking through the red. He was overdue for a color, which Jamie had told him time and again he could forgo, the signs of age sexy, but Aidan wasn't ready to let them show yet. Not in his hair nor in the gym nor in the stands, cheering him and his team on like a college kid. Including this weekend. "I love having you on the road with me for a change."

Aidan was frequently in the stands at their home games but work usually kept him in San Francisco when Jamie was on the road, especially this time of year. For this tourney, however, Cam had managed to shoo him out of the office. Jamie would have to thank his best friend again because the heated look in his husband's autumn eyes when he propped his chin on Jamie's chest and rumbled a "How much do you love it?" was highlight reel worthy.

Sliding his hands down Aidan's back and inside his jeans and boxers, Jamie grabbed his husband's ass and spread his cheeks, fingertips teasing his crack. Aidan moaned and squirmed, rutting his cock against Jamie. "I love it so much," Jamie said as he rocked back, "that I want to lay you out on this couch and fuck you while you're wearing nothing but my team's sweatshirt."

Aidan chased after his lips, nipped the bottom one, then drew back, batting his thick burnished lashes. "But what if we get come on it?"

"I think I know where to get you a new one. Or twenty," Jamie said with a wink. "Perks of fucking the assistant coach."

"In that case, do your worst, Coach Walker." The challenge in Aidan's voice, in his gaze, had been there since day one working together. *Impress me*, he'd told Jamie that day in the cyber division cave. Aidan's late husband had been an athlete; he knew better than most how to motivate Jamie. Then and now.

Keeping one hand on Aidan's ass, Jamie wrapped his other arm around his torso and levered up, twisting and shifting so Aidan landed on his back on the couch. Jamie stretched over him, indulging in a quick, plundering kiss, then escaping before Aidan could get his arms around his neck.

Aidan's "harrumph" as he flounced back onto the couch was epic.

"Don't pout," Jamie chided. "I'll be right back." Standing, he stripped out of his T-shirt, dropped his sweats, and grabbed the bottle of lube from the bedside table. "Your ass will thank—Fuck, Irish."

By the time Jamie had rotated back around, Aidan had shimmied out of his jeans and boxers and was rubbing his cock against his bare abs, just shy of the sweatshirt's hem. His autumn gaze that locked on Jamie's was molten. "Get over here and fuck me, Whiskey."

Jamie closed the distance in a single stride. Planting a knee between Aidan's spread thighs, he covered Aidan's body, their cocks hot and hard against each another, the scratch of the sweatshirt's lettering against Jamie's bare chest firing all his senses. Groaning, he crashed his mouth onto Aidan's, tongue sweeping in, tasting and taking, then surrendering as Aidan sucked on it shamelessly.

Making Jamie melt.

Then burning him hotter as he clasped their cocks in his hand and stroked.

Jamie gasped and shot out an arm, bracing himself against the back couch cushions. "Irish, you keep doing that, and this will be over before I get inside you." Despite his protest, he kept thrusting his cock against Aidan's, through his tight, slick grip, the heat and counter pressure driving him wild. Same as it always did when Aidan took control of the wheel.

"You won't." Aidan splayed his free hand in the center

of Jamie's chest and pushed him up. "Use that limber body and those long arms to get me ready. I want you inside me tonight."

Gritting his teeth, Jamie breathed deep—once, twice, a third time until the riot of blood and sensation coursing through him calmed enough to follow Aidan's orders. He opened the bottle of lube, coated his fingers, and shifted so he could reach behind the butt cheek Aidan helpfully lifted. He dipped his fingers into Aidan's crack he'd teased earlier.

"That's it, baby," Aidan panted.

Jamie pressed against Aidan's rim, easing one, then two fingers inside him, pumping and spreading, while Aidan kept the pace of his strokes relentless, building the pleasure for both of them. Pushing himself, it seemed, to the edge of control too. Sweat prickled his hairline, a bright red blush spread up his neck, and when Jamie stroked the soft spot inside him, his back bowed off the couch. "Fuck, Jamie. Fuck! Right there! Fuck, I love you."

Jamie gave in to the urge to lean forward, kissing away Aidan's mewl at losing his fingers. "Not long, baby, I promise. But I needed to kiss you. Needed you to taste how much I love you too." He claimed his mouth, their tongues and teeth clashing, wanting all of the man beneath him, none of it ever enough, even after all these years. "Always," he whispered against Aidan's lips, as he moved fully between his legs and pushed inside him.

"Always," Aidan echoed.

Repeated it again as Jamie took his cock in hand and stroked.

And again each time their speed picked up, racing toward their climax.

Until their rhythm faltered and Jamie erupted in the

tight, warm heat of his husband's ass, Aidan following him over the edge with a shout.

Jamie collapsed on top of his smiling husband, blissed out and not the least bit worried about the come-covered sweatshirt between them. He'd happily replace a thousand of them for all the moments like these with his husband.

FOUR

Aidan woke to the same soft sensations he'd fallen asleep to, Jamie's fingers carding through his hair, his chest rising and falling gently beneath the arm Aidan had thrown over it. The room was also still dark, Aidan's eyes taking longer to adjust in the near pitch-black, only the faint glow of the bedside clock casting any light in the room.

Five thirty, according to said clock.

Aidan snuggled closer to the warm body beside his. "I didn't wear you out enough to sleep to the alarm?"

Jamie's chuckle rumbled beneath his ear. "Watched too much tape. So many plays running through my head."

"You were great out there yesterday. Not just the plays we practiced but with the team too." He absently traced the interlocking N and C inked on Jamie's chest, debating whether to disturb the peace and quiet with the last thought he'd fallen asleep to. And the one that had woken him. But if there was one person in the world who he was completely safe with, who would listen and not judge, it was the man beside him. "Marsh noticed too," he said. "That you're good with the kids."

"I'm good at teaching them basketball. Otherwise, all the credit goes to my mom and sister, my niblings, and you."

"Me?" Aidan glanced up and met baby blue eyes smiling down at him.

"Yes, you." Jamie ducked his chin and dropped a kiss on his forehead. "Seeing how you are with Katie and the next-gen Talleys."

"Katie took to you right away."

"Katie also took to Nic. What does that tell you?"

Aidan laughed, remembering how his now ten-year-old niece had once been a tiny tyke who'd been his gruff best friend's "date" at his and Jamie's wedding. She'd been attached to "Uncle Nic" ever since, spending way more time at his brewery than was strictly legal for someone underage. Good thing said uncle was also the US Attorney for Northern California.

Jamie's hand drifted out of his hair to Aidan's arm over his chest, squeezing gently. "Talk to me, Irish."

Just as Jamie was the one person who he was completely safe with, he was also the one person Aidan could never hide from. He scooted closer, tightening his hold on Jamie's middle, unable to shake the sense his world was about to be upended. He'd had it all once before, then he'd lost it when Gabe had been killed. All these years later, reaching for more still felt like standing on the edge of a cliff. Like one wrong step, and he'd lose it all again. But in Jamie's arms— arms that had held him close for seven years, even when Aidan had pushed him away—maybe he could take that step. Maybe he could finally be brave enough to reach for more.

He swallowed. And stepped forward. "Marsh also asked if we'd thought about having any."

Jamie's breath caught and stiffness rippled through his frame. "Any?"

Aidan held tighter. "Kids," he said before he could chicken out. "Of our own."

"I think about it every time we step on a court together."

Aidan whipped his gaze back to his husband, Jamie's words the last thing he expected. "You do?"

"Of course," he said, as simply as he had last night about watching tape. "I wonder what it would be like to coach our own kids, to laugh and play and learn together." The tension ebbed from his frame, a smile touching the corners of his lips, reflecting the same one Aidan could feel turning up his own. "Assuming they like basketball. Or sports at all. And if not, we'll get one of our other friends to teach them to play chess. And we'll learn with them."

The image was so clear in Aidan's mind that he couldn't help but smile wider, but the next instant, his smile dimmed as he wondered how long Jamie had kept this to himself. "You should have—"

Jamie silenced him with a quick, soft kiss. "We have talked about it, and let me be clear, I don't need to have kids to feel whole. That burning need some folks talk about isn't there for me. Probably because we're surrounded by so many kids already. But it is something I think we'd be good at together. That I'd want to do with you, if you want that too."

"I do." The earth shifted with the truth, but rather than sinking, the sense of flying propelled Aidan up. He stretched and claimed the lips of the man who gave him courage this day and every day. "Maybe it's time we did something more than just talk."

Jamie's smile tasted like flying too.

Aidan would have liked to enjoy more of it, but a familiar knock on the hotel room door had him drawing back.

Jamie recognized it too. "Danny?"

"Sounded like it." Aidan unwound from Jamie and the sheets, flipped on the bedside light, and stood. He crossed to the dresser and checked his phone. "Yep, Daniel." His brother had texted twenty minutes ago asking if he was awake, and again five minutes ago to say he was headed over from the next-door luxury hotel where he and Mel were staying. "Just a second, baby bro," he called toward the door, then grabbed one of Jamie's tees from the drawer before snatching his jeans and boxers off the floor. When he turned back around, Jamie had also swung his legs off the bed and was halfway to standing. Hand to his shoulder, Aidan urged him back down. "I'll slip out and you can go back to sleep. Or keep running plays in your head. I can handle whatever this is."

"If he's here and it's still dark out, it's all hands on deck." Using his heft and extra inches, Jamie stood and forced Aidan back a step. "I'm gonna grab clothes and hit the bathroom right quick."

"Your top priority has to be the team, Jamie. You've got a game today."

"My top priority is you, *always*." Hand around his neck, Jamie swallowed any further objection with a kiss that made Aidan wobble on his feet. His next words only worsened the swooning. "And we're not done with this convo.

When the dust settles, we're gonna talk about more than maybes." Another quick kiss, then he slipped out from between Aidan and the bed, grabbed last night's no doubt crusty sweatshirt off the floor, and headed for the bathroom.

Following in his wake, Aidan flipped on more lights, grabbed Jamie the clean clothes he'd forgotten, and, once he'd handed them through the bathroom door to his husband, shut that door and opened the main one to the room.

In the hallway, his typically stylish brother looked uncharacteristically rumpled. "At least you knocked this time," Aidan said, referencing that early morning when Danny had used his lock-picking skills to break into the condo Aidan and Jamie had stayed at on their first assignment.

"At least you put on your own pants this time," Danny countered, reminding Aidan too of the state he and Mel had found them in, having hastily dressed in the dark to defend themselves against would-be intruders.

One of those "intruders," however, was missing this morning. "Where's Mel?"

"Got a call about a bounty," Danny said as he bustled into the room. "Sometime around two." Mel had recently gone full-time with Redemption Inc., the bounty hunter enterprise she ran with another of their family friends.

"Have you slept at all?" Aidan asked his brother, who was rolling his head around on his neck like a bobblehead doll.

Righting his gaze, he spread his arms wide. "Do I look like it?"

Jamie appeared out the bathroom and, clearly having

heard the exchange, made a beeline to the in-room beverage nook. "I'll get the coffee going."

Aidan leaned against the nearest wall and kept his attention on Danny. "Given the hour, I assume you're not here out of boredom or loneliness or to bring us a holiday surprise."

"Not the good kind. Owner of the stolen cargo had a tracker on it, but something or someone is blocking the signal."

Ah, now Aidan knew why Daniel was here. And so did Jamie, who stepped around Aidan and lightly squeezed his hip. "You finish the coffee. I'll wake the laptop."

Aidan lined up three cups as the cheap in-room coffeemaker gurgled to life. "You said the owner had shipped the diamonds with other luxury goods. Is he a collector or a reseller?"

"Bit of both."

"Since when is Talley Enterprises shipping for individuals?"

"We do it for Rafael Parsons, whose business also ships a quarter million tons of cargo with us per year."

A significant client whose trust Danny had to gain back.

"Anything else of his been stolen before?" Jamie asked.

"No, their cargo tends to be high-end luxury goods." Danny lowered himself on one end of the couch and rubbed a hand over his way-past-five-o'clock scruff, as visible a sign as any of the hours he'd been awake. He graciously accepted the mug of caffeine Aidan handed him. "Cargo theft is skyrocketing, especially as the holidays approach, but it's usually items the average person can afford. Handheld electronics and basic commodities like food and drinks."

"The price of everything's skyrocketing," Aidan said as he finished fixing his and Jamie's coffees.

"And everyone's willing to look the other way for a deal. This is the first one on us, at least partially."

"All right," Jamie said from where he'd set up at the table with his laptop. "I need specs on the tracking."

Danny pulled his phone out of his pocket and handed it to Jamie. Two sips of coffee later, he was deep into whatever it was hackers did. Aidan settled between them and turned his attention back to his brother.

"Did you check in yet with Rick or Matt?"

"Haven't had time. Aside from taking Mel to the airport, I've been on the phone with Siobhan and the owner's insurer all night, until I got a call from Parsons this morning, just before I texted you."

"Is that the first time you've spoken with Parsons since the goods were stolen?" At Danny's nod, Aidan asked, "So who were you talking to yesterday?"

"His executive assistant and the insurer. Parsons was traveling. They knew he had a tracker on the diamonds, but we couldn't get the details until Parsons made contact. Only he had that information."

Aidan glanced over his shoulder at Jamie. Brows pinched, fingers flying, he was fully absorbed in whatever was going on in that little black box on his screen. Aidan withdrew his phone and bought him some more time.

Rick answered after two rings. "This is Lorton." He sounded as tired as Danny looked, his Midwestern drawl more pronounced.

"Hey, Rick. It's Aidan. I'm here with Jamie and Danny." He flipped the phone to speaker. "Any leads on the truck?"

"I've got Matt here too," Rick answered. "We've been going through the surveillance video from the yard."

"Streaming it to you now," Matt said.

Aidan logged into his work server on his phone and scooted closer to Danny while the video loaded.

"That's the transfer," Rick narrated once the video started playing.

Two crates were being moved via forklift from a shipping container to a cargo van. As the forklift began to reverse, a commotion erupted, the group of kids—teenagers —Matt had mentioned yesterday crossing behind the lift.

"Hey, watch it!" one chided.

"Tonto del culo!" a different student called.

"Bruh!" a third shouted.

"Did you know about the students visiting?" Rick was asking Danny, but Aidan was stuck on the Spanish shout amidst the English ones, something about the voice vaguely familiar. He slid the cursor back and watched it again.

"You see something?" Danny asked.

He zoomed in but couldn't see any of the students' faces. And then they were gone, another truck pulling into frame and another forklift approaching with someone else's cargo.

"No. I thought maybe I could catch one of their faces." Aidan refocused on the certainty they did have. "What've you got on the truck?"

"Gate cams show one man behind the wheel," Rick said. "Darien White, according to facial recognition."

"Rap sheet?"

"Petty thefts, bar fights, meth bust that landed him in jail. He's currently out on parole."

"Which he's violating," Matt said, "given the last sighting of that truck was on the 125 in San Diego County."

"He's headed for the Otay border crossing," Danny said.

Aidan tended to agree. Truck full of goods, probably with forged papers, given the targeted nature of the theft. "Intercept?"

"San Diego field office has teams on the way."

"They're not going to find the diamonds."

Aidan spun toward Jamie. "You cracked the tracker?"

"Of course." Those words again, along with Jamie's sly smile, made Aidan want to laugh, but that was the last thing Danny needed right then. He internalized the admiration for his husband, who delivered exactly the information Danny did need. "The tracker is in LA." He rotated his laptop so they could see the blinking red light near the coast. "In a parking lot at El Segundo Beach."

"Someone's catching a nap," Rick said.

"Or found the tracker and pitched it there," Matt countered.

"Or is waiting to make a handoff at LAX," Aidan finished with the theories.

"I think Aidan's right," Jamie said. "Tracker's on the move, headed inland."

FIVE

The car junkie in Jamie had always dreamed about a high-speed chase through the streets of LA. Had seen it enough times in movies and on TV to imagine how it would go.

Predawn speeding down the interstate in a rented Outback was not the car chase of Jamie's dreams. Hell, they weren't even chasing anyone yet, and there weren't enough cars on the road to qualify for Bureau field training. The former LEO in him was glad for that. The amateur stunt driver was a little disappointed.

"Maybe ease up on the gas," Aidan gritted from the passenger seat beside him. "You're outrunning our backup."

He chanced a glance in the rearview mirror, confirming with his eyes what Aidan had told him. After a quick check forward, he chanced a glance at Aidan, confirming what the tone of his voice had also told him. Jaw tight, skin pale, Aidan was gripping the seat belt across his chest like his life depended on it. He still wasn't good with car chases of any variety. Fair, given his history with how they usually ended. Jamie itched to take his hand off the wheel and give his husband's thigh an encouraging squeeze, but that would probably only heighten Aidan's stress.

He eased off the gas instead and allowed the Bureau cruisers who'd joined them at the last major interchange to catch up, their lights flashing around the interior of the Outback. "Rick, any update?" Jamie asked of Aidan's colleagues on the other end of the open phone line. He and Matt were tailing their suspect in a black Charger with stolen tags toward LAX, as Aidan had suspected.

Or so they thought, until Matt swore.

Aidan leaned forward, white-knuckling the seat belt. "What's going on there?"

"They picked up the tail and diverted."

"Heading east on Imperial," Rick reported, the tracker's icon on the onscreen map confirming the same.

Aidan hit Mute. "I was wrong. More gas." Jamie hit the gas, and Aidan took them back off Mute. "Is it White behind the wheel? Is there anyone with him?"

"Only the driver in the car," Matt replied. "Heat signatures confirm. No positive ID, but by White's vitals, we should see his head over the headrest."

"We don't," Rick said before cursing too, his accent getting thicker by the second. "Exiting the freeway. North on Inglewood."

"Passing the exit for Western," Jamie called as they sped under the freeway sign.

"Take the next one onto Van Ness," Matt said. "Parallel us north."

"Confirmed," Jamie said, darting across lanes in time to exit. He slowed enough on the ramp for one of the cruisers with lights and sirens to take the lead through the intersection, clearing a path for them.

"We need to end this before they get into the neighborhoods or the cemetery," Matt said.

"We're headed toward the Forum," Aidan said. "Can we corner them in the parking lots there?"

"There or the stadium," Rick confirmed.

"Get someone on the horn," Matt called over the other radio to dispatch. "We need some gates opened."

By the time Jamie crossed the next intersection, three options had been identified, one settled on. "Left on West 108, Jamie," Rick said. "Then north on Crenshaw, then left on Pincay. One car will stay with you. The other is going to sweep north to Briarwood. Cut off the path there."

"Confirmed," Jamie said again, then hammered the gas, racing through Inglewood's streets, the lead cruiser's bright lights and loud sirens keeping their path clear. Before long, the sirens began to echo, Rick's and Matt's parallel path closing in. "It's almost over, Irish," Jamie said, keeping his eyes on the road and hands on the wheel but aware of Aidan's quickened breaths beside him. "Not long now."

The sun rose as they sped down Pincay, the sweeping angles of the gleaming oval stadium coming into view on the left, the storied red and white arena on the right, and dead ahead, a far-off vehicle quickly resolving into the black Charger they were all after. "Target in sight."

Then not, all sight momentarily gone, blotted out by the Charger's blinding high beams.

Aidan's "Oh god" threw Jamie back to an early morning in Galveston, Texas seven years ago. But unlike that morning when Jamie had had no idea of his surroundings, no backup, and limited room to maneuver, this morning was a different story. Just before being blinded, he'd glimpsed the familiar and relatively giant five-lane LA T-junction ahead, plus a cruiser flying down the intersecting street where one of the arena's gates had been opened. He could make this work.

Biting back the "Hold on" on the tip of his tongue, knowing that would hurtle Aidan even further back into the past, Jamie repeated his "Almost over" for Aidan, then hit the brakes, swinging the tail end of the Outback out and around. With a quick shift of the gears, he threw the car into reverse, the transmission making a grinding awful protest, but speed and inertia carrying them out of the way of the oncoming Charger and Rick's and Matt's cruiser. A blink later, Jamie's vision cleared, and he watched as the cruiser that had been behind them blocked the Charger's path forward, and with Rick and Matt on its tail, the Charger was forced left, into the path of the oncoming cruiser, the agent inside firing out the window at the Charger's tires. The Charger swung left, right into the parking lot where they wanted it.

By the time Jamie and Aidan caught up, Rick and Matt, together with their backup, had surrounded the Charger, all of the agents braced behind their doors, vests and safeties on. Jamie parked between two of the cruisers behind the Charger and obeyed Aidan's "Stay in the car." Not that he would risk the arrest by doing otherwise. Not his place anymore. But he did roll down the windows so he could hear what was going on.

"Hands where we can see them!" Matt shouted at the suspect, who must have complied, because Matt holstered his weapon and inched closer. "Where are the goods?"

"Trunk," came the reply, the voice masculine, but cracking . . . like a teenager's?

"Stand clear," Matt called to the other agents, then to the driver, "Open it."

The trunk popped open.

Jamie held his breath as Aidan approached the car. He reached into the trunk and removed a briefcase. The tracker icon on the phone's map moved farther away from the Charger with each step Aidan took back toward their vehicle.

"Tracker says that should be it," Jamie said as Aidan laid the briefcase on the hood. "Now, will the combo Parsons gave Danny work?"

Aidan spun the dials on the combination lock, and a click later, Aidan heaved a sigh of relief. "We got it." He closed the case, handed it through the window to Jamie with a small smile, then turned back to Matt and Rick.

And went rigid, every muscle of his back going stiff beneath the tee, vest, and FBI jacket he'd thrown on.

"Irish, what is it?"

No response.

Jamie glanced back out the windshield to where Rick was pulling the driver out of the Charger. Brown hair, light brown skin, lanky limbs, and clothes that were two sizes too big, the kid couldn't have been more than sixteen.

Aidan wavered on his feet, and Jamie bolted out of the car, orders be damned. Reaching Aidan's side, he wound an arm around his waist, steadying his worryingly pale husband. Was this about their conversation earlier? The topic of kids had been on their minds, but Aidan had handled juvenile cases before, and while yes, they could shake him up, Jamie had never seen him react like this. "Aidan, talk to me. You look like you've seen a ghost."

"I think I have," he said, voice a thready, pained thing, his autumn gaze trained on the stormy blue one glaring at him from beside the Charger. This wasn't about kids in general; it was about this kid in particular.

"You know him?" Jamie interpreted Aidan's silence as a yes. "Who is he?"

Aidan swallowed hard. "My godson, Angel Crane."

SIX

Two hours and a half dozen "I'm fine" replies later, Jamie stood on one side of the observation glass, his husband on the other. Inside the interrogation room, Aidan leaned against the far wall, his chin lowered but every muscle of his lean frame strung tight, flinching with each surly word Matt and Berat drew out of the suspect across the metal table from them.

Not just any suspect.

Aidan's *godson*.

Angel Crane.

"When we worked Gabe's case," Jamie said to Danny beside him, "I researched Tom, but I was so focused on his financials and the connection to his and Gabe's killer that I didn't make *this* connection."

"That his and Isabella's son was named after Gabriel?"

Jamie nodded, recalling those early days when he'd been newly assigned to the San Francisco field office. When he'd watched from afar at office parties while Mel, Aidan, and his Bureau partner, Tom, would circle up with Gabe and Isabella and exist in their own seemingly perfect world.

During the investigation, Mel had told him that Isabella otherwise stayed far away from their work, that Tom and Aidan protected her from all of it. But then her grandmother's immigration status had been used as leverage against Tom by the terrorist who'd ultimately killed him and Gabe. Who had tried to kill Aidan and Jamie, multiple times over, before meeting his own demise.

Aidan and Jamie had survived, Mel and Danny too, and they'd eventually gotten their happily-ever-afters, but what had happened to Isabella? And her and Tom's son? Nothing good, it seemed, according to sixteen-year-old Angel's rap sheet. He'd racked up an impressive number of speeding tickets, truancy calls, school suspensions, and a misdemeanor larceny. His actions today would add several felonies to the list.

Jamie dragged a hand down his face, wondering how the day had gone from damn near perfect, he and Aidan committing to plan for the next big step in their future, to the past rearing up and punching them in the face again.

A past that Jamie had only cursorily read over in Tom's file and that Aidan had rarely mentioned. He'd never mentioned that Angel was his godson. Because he didn't want Jamie to know? Or because Aidan had been cut out of Angel's life? The latter seemed more likely, and by the heavy set of Aidan's shoulders, he was deeply regretting his absence, involuntary or not.

"Did Mel get a location on Isabella?" Jamie asked Danny. They'd learned through official channels that Isabella was a flight attendant for a major airline. Those official channels were slower, however, than Mel's bounty hunter ones at pinpointing a current location for Angel's mother.

"Should be arriving in Paris soon."

"Where'd the flight originate from?"

"JFK," Danny replied. "Izzy worked the red-eye from LAX the night before."

Leaving Angel to his own devices. Jamie idly wondered how often. Could he hack into those same channels of Mel's to find out? Or directly into the airline's manifests? Jamie was still putting together mental to-do lists when Rick opened the hallway door and poked his head into the room.

"Danny, you got a sec to go through more port footage?"

Knowing it would be longer than a second, Jamie closed the door behind his brother-in-law and refocused on the interrogation.

"Did you know what you were stealing?" Matt asked.

"Or who it belonged to?" Berat added.

"I didn't steal nothing," Angel huffed, despite his public defender, Tricia Harris's, caution to remain quiet. "I was just taking that briefcase across town for a friend. I didn't know it was stolen."

"Then why'd you run from us once you spotted the tail?" Matt said. He was a cagey interrogator, nonreactive, almost flat, a stark contrast to his out of work personality.

"Because someone was tailing me."

"With flashing lights and sirens."

"Instinct," Angel sneered as he cut a glare at Aidan. With his tan skin, shaggy brown curls, and long dark lashes, his light blue eyes, burning bright with anger, were a startling focal point. "Doesn't usually end well for me."

"If you were just moving a briefcase," Berat said, "then what were you doing at the port yesterday?"

"Field trip."

"Except that wasn't your school class." The detective leaned forward. "Were you creating a diversion, or were you there to confirm the goods were on-site?"

"Don't answer that," Tricia said, and this time the kid listened. Either way, Angel's actions were coordinated, and he had no good explanation for them.

"If you tell us who you were supposed to meet at LAX," Matt said, eliciting a revealing flick of Angel's gaze, "we can make this easier on you."

"Or who you were working with at the port," Berat said. "Was it Darien White who told you the plan? Who handed the briefcase off to you? Did he get into another car afterward?" The San Diego field team had found the abandoned cargo truck five miles shy of the border checkpoint. Empty, with no White in sight.

"Felonies off the table?" Tricia asked.

"Not in my power to deal," Matt said, resting back in his chair. "But I can ask and recommend."

"Then you better go do that." Tricia wasn't backing down, which Jamie appreciated. Any LEO worth their salt would for the sake of justice. And in this case, he personally appreciated it, for Angel's and Aidan's sakes.

Hell, Jamie was surprised Aidan hadn't already put one of their several defense attorney friends on a private plane down here. Jamie knew firsthand the lengths Aidan would go to for family, even if they were estranged.

Even as Aidan was being eaten alive by guilt.

Jaw clenched, brows knitted over worried-sick eyes, Aidan hadn't taken his gaze off Angel despite the teen's stinging barbs. He waited for Matt and Berat to leave the room before asking Angel, "How did you get wrapped up in this?"

"What else was I supposed to do when you took everything from us?"

Angel's words were barely a whisper, but they landed like a grenade, Jamie's own balance momentarily shaken as he imagined the hole they'd ripped open in Aidan's chest. The next second, Jamie's legs were back under him, and his hand was on the doorknob, ready to throw it open and barge in to protect Aidan from another blow.

Aidan's gaze darted his direction, as if he could see him through the glass, as if he could sense him simmering just on the other side. He shook his head, once, and Jamie stopped short, coming back to his senses. His presence wouldn't help. Nor was it necessary, Angel's PD stepping in again and cautioning him against saying more. Angel pressed his lips together, and Aidan had apparently had enough too, pushing off the wall and walking through the door Jamie opened for him.

He closed it behind Aidan, clicked off the interrogation room speaker, then drew Aidan into his arms. He was stiff as a board, muscles coiled tight with adrenaline, breaths coming short and fast, on the verge of hyperventilating. Cradling his head in one hand, Jamie glided his other up and down Aidan's back, repeating the motion until Aidan's breaths slowed. Until eventually his muscles loosened, and he wrapped his arms around Jamie's waist.

"Thank you," he said after another couple minutes in each other's arms.

"I'm glad I was here."

Aidan gave him a squeeze before stepping out of his

hold. He turned and leaned against the wall beside the glass, looking back through it at Angel. "I'm not certain I wouldn't have punched a wall just now if you weren't. I'm glad for that. Less glad you're having to see this. That I let things get to this," he said with a futile gesture toward the glass.

"Talk to me, Irish." Jamie regretted the words as soon as they were out, a mirror of this morning's entreaty.

Broken now.

Aidan's answering laugh was harsh, as if scraping over its jagged edges. "Talk about a wake-up call." He raked a hand through his hair and left it cupped around his nape, head bowed. "How could I think—"

"Don't." Jamie closed the distance between them, his front to Aidan's back, his hands on his hips. "Don't connect the two. They're unrelated. Talk to me about *this*. About Angel."

Aidan dropped his hand and lifted his head, resting back on his heels and giving Jamie some of his weight. "After the investigation," he started, then paused, swallowing hard, as if the past were a lump lodged in his throat. "After all that, Izzy wanted nothing to do with me. Or with Mel. Or with any of us. She packed up Angel and moved down here to where the rest of her family had relocated."

"Did you try to make contact?"

"Once. Got a blue streak of Spanish curses for the effort. I'd never heard her so angry, and I'd known Izzy since my first day of school in the States. I also knew when she hung up the phone that day that I'd never hear from her again. That was it." He shook his head and leaned more heavily against Jamie. "I kept tabs on them for a while. Everything seemed fine. After a certain point, it felt like an invasion of their privacy, so I stopped." He lifted a hand toward the glass, like he wanted to reach through it to his estranged family on the other side. Jamie stopped him short, gently grasping his outstretched hand. Aidan's fingers clenched around his, hard enough to make Jamie wince. "I did this, Whiskey. I ruined his life."

"You did no such thing." Jamie curled their joined hands against Aidan's chest and wrapped his other arm around his waist, embracing him. "You are not responsible for his father's choices. Or for his mother's, or his own."

"He's just a kid."

"Exactly. Which is why the Bureau and LBPD will cut him a deal. You know how this works. They want the higher-ups. Angel's just a runner, and in this case, the stolen goods were recovered."

"And you know it's never that simple." Aidan tilted his head, temple pressed against Jamie's cheek. "Nice driving today, by the way."

"You didn't seem to enjoy it in the moment."

"I never enjoy it in the moment."

Chuckling, Jamie was relieved to feel Aidan do the same, but before he could turn him in his arms and check for a smile, the door behind them opened, and Danny leaned in. "I've got Izzy." He held his phone out to Aidan.

Aidan's temporary reprieve vanished, all of his earlier tension rushing back in. He straightened out of Jamie's arms, took the phone from Danny, and stepped to the far corner of the room, phone held to his ear. "Isabella."

Without the phone on speaker, Aidan was too far away for Jamie to hear more than Isabella's muffled, rapid-fire Spanish. But Aidan's words and body language, the way he closed in on himself again, made the mostly one-sided conversation clear enough.

"He's cooperating," Aidan told her. Not exactly true, but it was what Angel's mother needed to hear. "I don't know when he'll be released." Clearly not what she needed to hear, Izzy's voice escalating in volume. Aidan rushed to clarify. "His public defender is good, but I can have the best defense attorneys in San Francisco here by midafternoon." He closed his eyes, pain washing over his features. "You wouldn't have to pay for them, Izzy." Whatever she said next caused Aidan to slump against the wall, defeat a black cloud crashing down around him. "I'm sorry."

Jamie made to move, no door in his way to Aidan's side, but Danny's hand on his forearm stalled him. "Not yet."

"Right, okay," Aidan said after another moment. "I'll stay with him until you get here." A streak of lightning bolted through the storm cloud, Aidan's voice strengthening. "Isabella, I'm not leaving him alone in holding. I'm staying with him until you get here." She must have conceded to his one demand, Aidan nodding once as he pushed off the wall. "See you soon."

Danny released his forearm, and Jamie met Aidan halfway across the room, looping an arm around his waist as Aidan handed the phone back to Danny. "I'll update Mel," Danny said, then slipped out of the room.

"And I'll stay here with you," Jamie told Aidan.

"No, you won't."

"Aidan—"

He laid the pads of his fingers over Jamie's lips, silencing his objections. "You have a game today. You need to go do your job, Whiskey."

Hand around his wrist, Jamie lowered Aidan's, then wrapped it in his against his chest. "My job, my life, my top priority is you, Irish. Always."

"I can't be the reason you lose today. Not on top of everything else." The strain in his voice, the tension vibrating through his taut frame, was the last thing Jamie wanted to be the cause of. He had enough sources of stress already.

"Okay," he said as he stepped closer. "Your call." He pressed a soft, firm kiss to Aidan's lips, then rested their foreheads together, waiting for some of the tension to recede again. "But you call me if you need anything. If you need me to count breaths with you, or if you need me to tell you how much I love you. You are always my priority."

SEVEN

It was closing in on midnight when Angel uttered his first words to Aidan since their standoff in interrogation that morning. "Why am I not in gen pop at LBC?" Lying on a metal bench, he kept his gaze fixed on the ceiling, but seeing as they were the only two people in the holding cell corner of the LA field office, Aidan assumed the question was for him.

He threw a question back at his godson as he continued to air toss the foam Santa toy he'd grabbed off the guardsman's desk. "There a reason you needed to be in gen pop there?" Someone else he was working for? Had that been the real play? Yes, Angel was his godson, but Aidan was still an agent. And concerned for said godson, whether Angel wanted it or not.

"Nope," he said, popping the *p*. "Just wondering why I got a metal bench in here instead of there."

"How do you even know what *gen pop* means?"

"I watch movies."

Aidan leaned back in the rickety desk chair that had

molded to his ass hours ago and kicked his feet up on the corner of the observation desk. "You're not in gen pop because you're a kid."

Angel turned to glare at Aidan, his blue eyes so much like his father's that a shiver raced up Aidan's spine. His voice, when it cracked low, sounded like Tom's too. "I'm not a kid."

"Let me rephrase," Aidan said, ignoring the ghost in the room for the very real human in front of him. His godson, who'd grown into even more of a beanpole than he'd been at age nine, his gangly limbs loosely hanging off the bench in the oversize jeans and hoodie he wore. "You're a minor."

"My minor ass has been in gen pop before."

Aidan set the toy down and raked a hand through his hair as he made a mental note to dig into Angel's rap sheet. Have Jamie dig further and find out what chaos he'd missed the past six years. If there was anything Aidan could do to still some of that chaos, he would, because despite what Jamie said, Aidan couldn't help but think that yes, he was responsible for the situation, at least in some part. "You're not in gen pop because the Bureau would like you to cooperate and because you're the godson of a Bureau SAC."

Angel scoffed. "Special Agent in Charge now?" He cocked a bushy brow before he rotated his head back to stare at the ceiling. And threw another verbal hook like he had earlier that morning. "My dad's death get you that?"

Hurt just as badly as it had that morning too. "Angel—"

"Saw you got a hot new husband too. Some basketball star."

"Jamie, and he's a coach now."

"So it was just me and Mom who lost everything while

you got a promotion and another rich athlete husband. Got it."

If Aidan could disappear into the chair, he would, the guilt crushing, whether it was misplaced or not. The only thing that kept him upright was the tiny bit of himself that wanted to argue, like he would with Angel's dad when they'd been Bureau partners. Like Jamie would for him if he were still here. He'd remind Aidan how he'd almost lost himself in a bottle after the accident, how he'd almost lost his own life in that crash too and had pins in his arm that kept the survivor's guilt forever fresh, how he, Jamie, Mel, and Danny had all almost lost their lives during their quest to solve Tom's and Gabe's murders.

Because that was what they'd been. Murders.

But this wasn't a competition, and Aidan was fairly certain Angel and the guilt would win if he went down that road. He deflected instead. "And you got a lead foot out of it."

Angel shrugged, insolent in the way only teens could pull off.

"Future bit of advice," Aidan said. "You can't outdrive Jamie. No one can."

Angel swung his legs around off the bench and dragged himself upright. "How did he—" He slammed his lips shut, wanting to ask but refusing to engage.

"Ask him yourself sometime," Aidan said, throwing out a breadcrumb. Maybe he'd engage with Jamie, if not with him. He added another to the trail. "He was an agent for a while too. Still holds the Bureau road course record."

Angel slumped against the wall, arms folded, his over-long curls falling over his long face. He looked more like a lost kid than he had all day.

Aidan lowered his feet and stood, feeling every pin in his arm and every one of his forty-nine years. Circling the desk, he stepped over to the cell and leaned against the bars. "Angel, what happened?"

"My lawyer said not to talk to you about the case without her."

"I don't mean about the case." The words came out harsher than intended, colored by a long day of frustration and guilt. But all those emotions were directed inward, none of them at the kid across the cell from him. Aidan softened his tone and tried again. "I mean with you and Izzy. Last I checked, the two of you were doing well. You had family here."

"They turned their backs on us too." He lifted that haunting blue gaze. "Probably about the time you stopped checking."

"I didn't want to."

"You still did," Angel said, enough of a breadcrumb in his words, in his bitter, hurt tone, to keep Aidan engaged too.

"I'm not going to now."

EIGHT

Unlike last night, Jamie was mostly asleep when the click of the hotel room lock nudged him toward awake. But only slightly. He stayed in that halfway dozing space while Aidan moved around the room, unloading his pockets, ditching his clothes, then using the bathroom before sliding into the bed behind Jamie, the big spoon to his little one. "He sleeps."

"Not well without you." Jamie snagged his arm and pulled it the rest of the way over his hip, hauling Aidan closer. "What time is it?"

"Just after one."

"Isabella get in?"

"Eventually, after some weather delays."

"What—"

Aidan kissed the back of his shoulder. "Tell me about the game. Did you win?" Another kiss. "Or did you lose? Is that why you're finally sleeping?"

"We won," Jamie said with a small smile that stayed in place even as he added, "We'll lose tomorrow, though."

Aidan gave his behind a gentle knee tap. "Ye of little faith."

"Me of reality." He rolled over under Aidan's arm, biting back the wince that wanted to escape when he glimpsed Aidan's long, tired face. He pushed his top strands back instead and trailed his fingers over the red and silver stubble dotting his jaw. He also ignored the conversation he wanted to have in favor of the one Aidan seemed to need, for now. "Would I love for us to win tomorrow? Yes. But we're playing the future national champions."

"You can't know that."

Jamie leveled his husband with the knowingest glare he could muster at one in the morning.

Aidan chuckled. "Fine, but tonight was a good game?"

"One of the best." Jamie's smile grew wider. "Won by twenty."

"That's good, baby." Aidan scooted closer, tucking his head under Jamie's chin, nuzzling his throat, and burrowing closer. Jamie recognized the behavior, something Aidan was prone to do after particularly rough days at the office. Jamie held him tight, letting the silence wash over them, letting Aidan take the comfort he needed. There were plenty of days Jamie missed working for the Bureau, missed being Aidan's partner at work too, but there were more days when he was glad he could be this for Aidan, a quiet, separate port in the storm. He was almost back to sleep when he felt more than heard Aidan's words. "I'm sorry about earlier at the station."

"You don't need to apologize for how you feel. This was all a shock."

"For you too. I should've told you—"

The last thing Aidan needed to do was apologize to him.

He shifted so Aidan was on his back, Jamie stretched along his side, head resting on his folded arm beside Aidan's on the pillow. With his other hand, he lightly coasted his fingers over Aidan's chest, over his heart. "You didn't want to rip open a wound you'd barely stitched together. One you didn't want to create. I'm not gonna hold that against you."

"But I still should've—"

Mirroring Aidan's gesture from earlier in the day, Jamie pressed his fingers against Aidan's lips, then waited for him to turn his head and meet his gaze. "If Izzy hadn't cut you out, would you have introduced me to them?"

"Of course," he mumbled against Jamie's fingertips.

Jamie lowered his hand and draped his arm over Aidan's chest. "Then stop beating yourself up over something you couldn't do."

"Don't logic me when you're still half asleep."

"I'm good like that." Jamie smiled and snuggled closer, pulling Aidan half under him the way Aidan liked.

"You are good," Aidan said and dropped a kiss on his forehead. He fidgeted into position, then, after another minute, stilled. Jamie thought he'd dozed off until he spoke again, quiet in the dark. "I think Angel would like to know how you pulled that maneuver in the Outback."

Jamie chuckled on the edge of sleep. "I don't think we want to teach him that." Then recalled something else he wanted to remind Aidan of before he drifted the rest of the way to sleep. "Not our kids either."

Aidan's "Eventually" sounded like hope to Jamie's ears.

NINE

Aidan woke slowly, noticing first the absence of Jamie's big, warm body draped over his, then detecting the scent of not-hotel-room coffee and . . . chorizo? He eked open his eyes, unsurprised to find Jamie at the table by the couch, unloading foil-wrapped logs from a paper bag. "Did you get breakfast burritos again?"

Jamie grinned over his shoulder, then stepped around the table and pulled back one of the blackout curtains, leaving only the willowy sheer drape to filter the morning light. "The food truck is *right there*," he said, pointing out the window.

Aidan laughed as he pushed himself upright. "You act like you live somewhere that doesn't have food trucks on every corner."

"Fine," he said with a shrug and a smirk. "I'll eat your burrito too."

"Don't you dare." Aidan snagged his sweats off the floor and dragged them on as he stood. He grabbed his phone off the charger, checked for texts and emails, and, seeing none he needed to answer immediately, made a beeline to the bathroom.

When he joined Jamie back at the table, his husband was halfway through his burrito, holding it in one hand and spreading file folders across the table with the other, each folder a different color.

As he bounced on the balls of his feet.

And why had the in-room coffeemaker been in the bathroom?

He glanced past the table at the couch—a Jamie-sized dent in the cushion—then up at his husband again, his eyes caffeine wide and his long caramel-colored top strands more unruly than usual. "How long have you been at it?"

"Since four," Jamie said around a bite. "Couldn't sleep. Then I killed all the coffee pods. So I had to go get us some more this morning. Which fine, fuck yeah, it's holiday blend time." He happy danced where he was standing. "And I needed sticky notes. And then the burritos"—he pointed at the window again—"were right there."

Yep, he was in full-on hacker mode.

"Game prep or the case?" Aidan asked as he claimed the other coffee and took a long sip. Jamie regularly traveled with the rainbow folders he lived and died by for organization, thanks to an agent they'd met in Texas. But if this had been game prep, the folders would be full of printouts. Not scribbled on yellow paper from a legal pad and sticky notes.

"Case," Jamie said, as he shoved the last bite of burrito into his mouth. "I couldn't do nothing."

Aidan was going to ask him to consult, officially, but after the game today. Unsurprisingly, the hacker couldn't wait. Aidan took another sip of coffee, then began peeling back the foil around his burrito. "What've you got?"

"Izzy," he said, nudging the blue folder. "Angel," the green one. "Cortez Family." Yellow. "White." Orange. "Parsons." Red. "We don't have a printer, obviously, and I wasn't going to trust the hotel one, so it's mostly just prelim work for you to follow up on."

"You didn't have to—"

"I'm going to be tied up most of today with media, practice, the game, then media again. I needed to do something to help." He pitched his cup in the trash can and began moving around the room, changing out of his sweats and into a suit as he talked. "Each of the folders corresponds to a file I set up on our private server. Sticky notes correspond. Everything I couldn't print out."

Aidan slid onto the couch and drew the folders closer, unsure where to start. "Highlights?"

"If you don't strangle Izzy's family, I might."

He pulled the yellow folder closer. "Angel said they cut them off. Right about the time I stopped checking on them."

"I don't think it had anything to do with you." He strode back across the room and handed Aidan his phone. "Just a sample of his uncle's browser history then."

Aidan didn't need to click on the links to know where they led. The names were enough. Right-wing news outlets and podcasts. Homophobic and transphobic talking heads. Evangelical interest groups and mega churches. A fucking conversion camp.

"Fuck." Aidan propped his elbows on the table and scrubbed his hands over his face. "He said you were hot." A throwaway comment yesterday that Aidan hadn't thought the least bit out of the norm, all of his family accepting, most of his friends queer, but his family, blood and found, were the exception.

"I think Izzy cut them off to protect herself and her son." Jamie pushed the blue folder in front of him before turning and continuing to put himself together for the day. "She's doing okay. Works too much but she's never missed a rent payment, has a good credit score, pays for Angel's private school, and is actually starting to save, probably for Angel's college."

"He's got the grades for it?"

"In science and math. Never makes less than an A."

Aidan reached for the green folder, reading over the lines of grades on a stray sheet of legal paper, nothing less than a B- anywhere in the rows.

"Got that from his godfathers, apparently."

Smiling, Aidan shook his head. "Not only. His mom too. Izzy was the only reason I passed geometry." He riffled through the other sheets of paper and notes. He didn't see White's or Parsons's names anywhere, nor the names of any other criminal figures or groups Aidan knew to be associated with cargo theft. "How'd he get tangled up ferrying stolen cargo?"

"That's what I couldn't sort." He swung by to reclaim his phone and pushed the orange and red folders forward. "Angel's got no connection to White or Parsons that I found on first search."

"What about the prior larceny? Angel said he'd been in gen pop before."

Jamie winced, and Aidan knew he wasn't going to like the answer. "He tried to shoplift his mom's wedding ring from the pawn shop she sold it to."

His stomach tumbled the egg, sausage, and coffee in it.

"Fuck. Fuck!" He moved to scrub his hands over his face again, but Jamie stopped him, fingers wrapping gently around his wrists.

"Don't go there," he said as he slid onto the couch beside him. "That was three years ago. She's back on her feet now. Angel too, even if he doesn't want you to think that."

He curled his hands around Jamie's, soaking in some of his steadiness while Aidan felt anything but. "What about the truancy and suspensions?"

"He's a queer, Latino kid at a Catholic school. Probably too smart for his grade, so he's bored out of his mind."

"Was it the same for you?"

"I'm white, that's a privilege Angel doesn't have, but make it a small southern town, giant county school, and yeah, I can relate to most of it. If not for the diner and basketball, that could have easily been me." He looped an arm around Aidan's shoulders, giving him more of that steadiness he needed. Aidan was sure Jamie would stay by his side all day if Aidan asked him to, but he'd already done more than expected, especially when there was a whole team depending on him today who needed his steadiness too. He laid a hand on Jamie's thigh. "Thank you for all of this, but you need to get to work."

"I know." Jamie laced their fingers together and gave him a quick kiss. "And so do you. You got enough to go on here?"

He jutted his chin at Angel's file, then at White's and Parsons's. "The thing that doesn't make sense. Angel has no connection to them."

"Exactly." Jamie stood, and, using their joined hands,

hauled him up too. "Now go be Agent Talley and solve the case."

"Yes, Coach."

That earned him a swat to the ass and another kiss, this one a little longer, a lot more lingering, before Jamie drew back and held his face in his hands. "You'll get through this. *We* will. And we'll get Izzy and Angel through it too."

TEN

The conference room door swung open, and Aidan glanced up from the printouts he was filing into Jamie's colorful folders. Dressed in jeans and a horrifically glorious ugly sweater, Agent Kim was the picture of holiday harassed, all the way to the grimace that turned down the corners of his mouth.

"Not one word about the sweater," he said as he yanked off the lime green, orange, and beige tiger-adorned tufted travesty and tossed it in a chair. "Breakfast with the family this morning." He pushed up the sleeves of the shirt he'd had on underneath. "Then on my way here I had the loveliest phone call with the prosecutor on Angel's case."

Not lovely at all judging by his tone. "He wouldn't budge?"

Matt dropped into the chair across from him. "Not without more."

"Angel's just a kid."

"With a record." Matt held up one finger. "Who committed a felony." Held up a second.

"Superficial," Aidan said, waving them away. "Both counts."

Matt leveled him with his dark gaze. "Not everyone is besties with their local US Attorney." And didn't flinch at Aidan's answering glare. "Facts, Talley." He wasn't wrong, said bestie of Aidan's married to Matt's former Bureau partner, who was Jamie's best friend. Yes, it was a tangled web that usually worked in Aidan's favor. None to be had here, it seemed.

"Do I need to call said bestie?" It wouldn't be the first time Nic had flexed outside his jurisdiction.

Matt shook his head. "Save the juice for a battle you can win. Rooster won't budge."

"Rooster?"

"Henry Roos," Matt explained. "The AUSA assigned to Angel's case."

"Is his last name the only reason he's called Rooster?"

"Unfortunately not," Rick said as he entered the room. "He's got the big hair, puffed-out chest, and strut to match." If the maybe-former model with a headful of blond waves and a chest almost as broad as Jamie's was saying that about someone else, Aidan could only imagine the prosecutor they were up against, confirmed as Rick carried on. "He's also meaner than any of the real roosters we have on the farm back home."

"Lovely." Just what Aidan needed on a case that mattered more than most, at least to him. "So, then, we need to get Angel talking."

"Which Tricia won't let him do without a deal."

"There's a tipping point for everyone." Leverage. Aidan had used it before to turn suspects into sources. "We need to solve for why."

Matt nodded to his folders. "That what you've been printing all morning?"

"A certain consultant went hacking for us overnight." Aidan spread the folders out, same as Jamie had done that morning, then spent the next twenty minutes walking Matt and Rick through Jamie's findings and the connections they'd already drawn that morning.

And those they'd noted were absent.

"So," Matt said, after Aidan finished the overview, "if it's not financial distress driving Angel's actions, what then? He did it for kicks? He's acting out?"

"Can't be dismissed," Aidan admitted. "He is a teenager, but I don't think that's it. When you go back through his record, those suspensions, the truancies, the larceny even, there's a reason for his actions. Despite what he wants us to believe, he's not a kid who acts out."

"Drugs, then?" Rick said. "Causing him to act out of the norm?"

Matt shook his head. "Test results came back negative for any controlled substances. Kid didn't even have caffeine in his system."

Pushing back from the table, Aidan stood and walked to the whiteboard he'd started scribbling notes on, three parties listed at the top.

Parsons. White. X.

Then two underneath them.

Angel. Y.

"Where's the connection?" he said. "Or better yet, who?" Aidan tapped a knuckle against the *Y*, one of two unknown variables on the board, but, he sensed, the more important one to Angel. "Y is someone Angel knows, and that person knows one or more of them," he said, pointing at the top line. "Any word on White?" he asked Rick.

"Still no sightings."

"As for Parsons," Matt said, "no known connections to White or Angel. He's cooperated fully and is conducting an in-house investigation to find out who might've leaked the shipment contents. So is Danny on the Talley side."

Aidan drew a single hash mark through Parsons's name. Not a full exoneration yet, but he agreed, it seemed Parsons was a victim more likely than a suspect. "We need to find White."

"He's due to check in with his parole officer tomorrow morning," Rick said. "He knows to alert us if he does."

They were halted from speculating any further by a knock at the door. "Come in," Matt called, once Aidan had moved to stand in front of the board.

The weekend receptionist who'd greeted him that morning stuck her head in the room. "Tricia Harris is here. Interrogation room two with Angel."

"We'll be right there," Matt said, then to Rick, "Keep digging."

Aidan circled the table, meeting Matt by the door. "Let's go get him to talk."

They'd barely closed the interrogation room door when Tricia made it clear how difficult that would be. "Do we have a deal?" she demanded.

"We're working on it," Matt replied.

"Well, until you have it, he's not talking."

He was looking as ragged as Aidan felt this morning —bloodshot eyes, pale skin, his curls gone flat. If Aidan had to guess, Angel had gotten even less sleep than him last night. Unsurprising, as his options had been a metal bench or the cement floor. He wore the clean clothes Izzy had brought for him, but given his otherwise drawn appearance, the slacks and button-up looked more ill-fitting than yesterday's jeans and hoodie.

"The AUSA isn't going to dismiss a felony without something in return," Matt said, continuing to volley with Angel's PD.

"But he's willing, if there is something?"

"It's Rooster, Trish. Of course he'll make a deal." The slip of a nickname, of Matt's usual formality in the interrogation room, made Aidan do a double take, but before he had time to ask what that was about, Angel lobbed a new grenade into the mix.

"I don't care about no deal."

"Angel, we should—" Tricia started, only to be cut off by her client.

"No," he said, voice sharp. Uncompromising. "I'm not talking. No deal."

"Because you do care about someone," Aidan said, and Angel's gaze snapped to him.

"Agents," Tricia said, standing. "Can we have a moment outside, please?"

Matt rose, but Aidan remained seated, gaze still locked with Angel's. "Whatever it is, whoever it is, we can help."

"Like I believe you," he said with a sneer, yesterday's default still in effect, but beneath the anger, distrust, and hurt, Aidan also detected exhaustion, worry, and a quiet hum of desperation.

Playing into that, he slid out of his chair and around to Angel's side of the table, kneeling beside his godson. He almost reached for his knee but caught himself, afraid to overplay his hand. "I told you last night, I'm here for you now. And I'm not going anywhere."

"We—" As fast as he'd snapped his gaze to Aidan's before, Angel jerked his chin the opposite direction now. "I'm fine," he corrected.

He was done talking. For now. But Aidan carried that telling slip—*we*—into the hallway with him. Angel wasn't done talking for good, and Aidan used that against Tricia's very valid "This is a conflict of interest."

"You heard him just now, right?" he said. "I am—"

"The best chance of getting him to talk. Yes, I heard that too." She ruffled her brown bangs with a heavy sigh. "I maybe even agree with you," she conceded. "But if this backfires, Rooster will have all our asses." She gestured between the three of them, then turned back toward the interrogation room, pausing at the door. "I'll work on Angel. Spell things out, legally, so he understands the consequences next time you talk."

"Which leaves us," Aidan said, "to find out who the other part of *we* is."

ELEVEN

Jamie had just filled the kitchen sink with soapy water when Danny and Mel strode in from the balcony of the Manhattan Beach condo they were borrowing, Aidan on their heels. "As much as I'd like to stay here and watch the waves all night," Mel said, "we've got a plane to catch." She had brought the jet back from wherever bounty duties had taken her, but only for a few hours to catch up with them on the case and pick up her husband.

"Are you going all the way home tonight?" Aidan asked her while Danny disappeared into the master suite to retrieve the briefcase of diamonds out of the safe where Aidan had secured it.

"Overnight in Vegas, then to SFO in the morning. I'm sorry I can't stay and talk to Isabella."

"I think less is more right now," Aidan said. "She said two words to me—'Get out'—when she arrived. I'll try again in the morning before we meet with the AUSA."

"She hasn't told the PD to boot you from the case yet,"

Jamie said as he rounded the dining bar. "That's a good sign."

Danny reemerged, briefcase in hand. "Well, once I get these back to Parsons tonight, civil charges will be off the table."

"Every little bit helps," Aidan said.

At the door, Danny hugged his brother, then hugged Jamie too, patting his back with a "Sorry about the game, bro."

The condolences were appreciated but unnecessary. "As I told Aidan, we played the future national champions. I'm just pleased our guys played as hard as they did and kept it close."

Aidan coasted a hand over his back. "I'm sorry I missed it. I heard it was a good game."

"I've got the tape," Jamie said with a wink.

"You need a lift back?" Mel asked him. "I can send the plane tomorrow."

He shook his head. "Those were our last games before exams, so I've got some time off before we start to prep for post-holiday games." He gestured at their surroundings. "And, thanks to Press"—one of his former players who now played in LA—"a place to crash while he's on the road."

"Try to enjoy it a little," Mel said, a hand on his forearm, then repeating the gesture with Aidan but lingering longer. "Don't be too hard on yourself."

"I keep telling him that," Jamie said.

"Make sure he believes it."

"Count on it," Jamie said, kissing her cheek, then locking up behind her and Danny. By the time he returned to the kitchen, Aidan was already elbow-deep in soapy water. "Let me take care of that so you can go to bed."

"Don't tempt me," Aidan said with a weary chuckle that matched the deep lines around his eyes and the raked-through strands of his hair. "And besides, you've had just as little sleep as I have the past few days." They worked in easy silence, Aidan washing, Jamie drying, until Aidan drained the sink and stole the dishtowel from Jamie to dry his own hands. "Thank you," he said. "For calling in the favor with Press, for staying, and for agreeing to talk to Angel tomorrow."

Jamie settled a hand in the small of his back. "Thank you for letting me. There's nowhere else I'd rather be." Then lowered that hand to lightly spank Aidan's ass. "Go light up the fire pit, and I'll bring you coffee. Or whiskey? I grabbed a bottle on the way over."

"Whiskey in my coffee."

"Yes, Irish," Jamie said with a chuckle of his own.

As Aidan shuffled his feet on the way back out to the balcony, Jamie grabbed two pods of decaf and poured two shots of whiskey in Aidan's mug. While he waited for the coffee to brew, Jamie accessed their private server from his phone and opened the Project Angel file from seven years ago. Named then after Aidan's late husband, Gabriel. Jamie had had no idea how relevant it would be again all these years later. He scrolled back through the information on Tom Crane he'd collected. Minimal, and only in connection with either Renaud, the terrorist they'd been tracking, or the work he and Aidan had done. He didn't think the former relevant, Renaud dead and his network dismantled, but it was possible the latter could turn up leads in the present. He initiated a search—Darien White against any of the cases Aidan and Tom had worked—then pocketed the phone and took their cups of coffee out to the balcony.

"Tell me about Tom," he said as he lowered onto the couch beside Aidan. "And not what's in our files but about him. Your friend." He waited until the momentary wobble of Aidan's hand stilled before he handed Aidan his mug. "Anything I can use when I talk to Angel tomorrow." After the small opening that Aidan had told him about, they'd decided to try and create a larger one out of Angel's curiosity about Jamie's stunt driving. But Jamie would need more than just an interest in wheels and how to use them to get the teen talking. Yes, they had cars in common, and certain other things too, including the loss of a parent. But Jamie wanted to know more about that parent beyond what was in his and the Bureau's files on Tom Crane.

More than all that, he sensed Aidan needed to talk about Tom too, about the good parts of their partnership, about the friend who'd been at his side since the Academy. And while it was slow going at first, Aidan seeming to drag the memories out of a locked box buried under a mountain of betrayal, once the stories began to flow and the whiskey loosened his tongue, Aidan was soon regaling him with the trouble the five of them—him, Tom, Gabe, Izzy, and Mel— used to get up to. Including one story about when Isabella was in labor. He and Tom and Gabe had eaten their way through an entire hospital vending machine, a bet Mel had made them so they'd stop pestering Isabella's doctors.

Jamie stretched an arm behind him, laughing. "Mel knew how to handle y'all way back then."

"Always." He leaned into Jamie's side and sipped the last of his Irish coffee. "If she'd been able to haul a fixer-upper and all of Tom's mechanic's tools into the hospital parking lot, she would have."

"Tom worked on cars?"

Aidan nodded. "Mostly restorations that he'd then donate to charities to auction off. I suppose that's where Angel picked it up."

"Same with me and my dad," Jamie said. "I was younger than Angel when he died, but I remember sitting on his workbench, watching him and hoping that one day I'd be tall enough to get under the hood."

Aidan hummed but didn't say more, and when Jamie glanced down a minute later, it was just in time to catch the mug from falling from a half-asleep Aidan's grip. Smiling, Jamie placed both empties on the fire pit ledge, then, hand under Aidan's knees, scooped him off the couch.

Aidan grumbled even as he burrowed into his chest. "This is unnecessary."

"Shut up," Jamie teased. "You like it."

The lack of further protest proved his point and proved Aidan was nearly out until he set Aidan on the bed. His husband's eyes were open and swirling with a mix of love and appreciation that sent Jamie to his knees between Aidan's.

"Thank you for tonight," Aidan said as he softly brushed Jamie's cheek. "I needed that. It felt good to remember the happy times, to remember the kind of man he was before it all went to shit. If I—" He swallowed hard, seeming to lose his words.

"If you what, baby?"

"If I start to shut down again, if I try to push you away, don't let me."

The Aidan of seven years ago had done exactly that when the connection between them had sizzled bright and hot, too soon after Aidan had lost the first love of his life. Scared, he'd pushed Jamie away, and the Jamie of seven years ago had let him. Neither of them were the same people now. Jamie wouldn't let go, and Aidan could depend on that persistence. "I won't," Jamie said, brushing their lips together. "And I also won't let you use this to convince yourself you wouldn't be a wonderful dad if you want to be."

Aidan lowered his chin, gaze averted. "I screwed up, Jamie. I took my eyes off the ball and missed half the game. If that were to happen with our own kids—"

"You were put in the penalty box, Aidan. Not by your choice."

Brown eyes peeked up at him through burnished lashes. "You're mixing sports metaphors."

"Because you were using bad ones to start." Aidan's huff of laughter was welcome, as was his upturned face and lowered shoulders. Jamie mimicked his earlier movement, cupping his cheek. "I'm not gonna push, Irish. Not in the middle of all this. But hear me when I tell you one does not reflect on the other, not in this case. You'd be a wonderful father, and when we're done with this case, we'll pick up the topic again."

"Yes, Coach," he said with a sly smile. "You know, if we have kids, we're gonna have to sneak around to have sex like we used to in the early days."

Jamie tilted his head toward the living room they'd just come from. "You wanna go back out there to the balcony?"

Aidan grabbed his shirt and tugged, pulling Jamie onto

the bed then rolling over him. "I think I'd rather just take you here." He captured Jamie's lips, the connection between them now, forged by years of love and trust, sizzling brighter and hotter than ever.

TWELVE

Aidan opened the door to the conference room and found Isabella standing by the window, staring out across the freeway at the National Cemetery. Her silver and brown curls were pulled into a low ponytail, her dark suit sharp, her arms folded, back straight, and head held high. A different woman than the one who'd flown two red-eyes, then a third long-haul to make it home to her son, only to trudge into holding with coffee stains on her uniform and find Aidan there waiting. The last person she'd wanted to see right then, even though he'd warned her he would wait. He'd kept his word and hadn't taken her *Get out* that night personally.

Would today's reception be any different? Fifty-fifty shot. "Isabella."

She turned from the window and didn't react with anger. A good sign. Low-level worry pinched her features, not the thrumming, exhausted kind of Saturday night, but rather the typical parent kind Aidan was used to seeing from his siblings, especially when any of them tried to get their kids to dress up. "Angel behaving?" she asked.

"He's fine. Grumbling about the suit." A small smile; Aidan counted it another win. "We wanted to talk with you a moment."

"We?"

Jamie entered the room behind him. "Izzy, this is my husband, Jamie. Jamie, this is Isabella."

"Ma'am, Jameson Walker, it's a pleasure to meet you." The extended hand, the wide easy smile, the accent always seemed to charm folks. Or maybe it was the compassion and sincerity wrapped around every word Jamie spoke. "I know it's been some time, but I'm sorry for your loss."

"Thank you." She withdrew her hand and folded her arms back across her chest. Her voice was polite but neutral, an underlying chill that was so unlike her that Aidan almost did a double take. "Are you with the FBI too?"

"No, ma'am. I coach basketball. But I used to be an agent, and I help out on cases from time to time." Aidan didn't think Isabella knew about Jamie's involvement in Tom's case. There'd been no trial afterward, only the aftermath. And she hadn't recognized Jamie's name. While her son had been keeping tabs on Aidan, it seemed Isabella really had tried to move on and leave the past behind. The realization hurt, but if it was what she'd needed, Aidan couldn't begrudge her. He'd done the same. And this morning, that disconnect could work in their favor.

Aidan gestured toward the table. "We think Jamie may be able to help with Angel's case, if you're willing to listen." Her dark gaze bore into his; Aidan didn't look away. "Please, Izzy. We just want to get Angel out of this." The stare down continued another few tension-filled moments until Izzy moved to the seat at the head of the table. Aidan claimed the chair to her right, Jamie on his other side. "Did Tricia explain to you why we're meeting here instead of at the courthouse?"

"She said she may be able to get Angel a deal."

"*If* he cooperates," Aidan said. "He hasn't told us who gave him the stolen goods to deliver or who he was supposed to deliver them to. Cargo theft is a top priority for the US Attorneys' Office and for the Bureau, especially here in LA. Either piece of info will lead them to the targets they're really after and get Angel out of the felony charge."

"But he won't talk." She sighed and ran a hand over her head, nails raking through the curls. "Welcome to my hell."

From Aidan's other side, Jamie rose, grabbed one of the bottles of water, and set it beside Izzy. "Has he been closed off since his dad's death?"

"Not exactly. It tore him up for sure, but he was better for a while after we moved here." She cracked the bottle of water open and took a long swallow. "He came out to me as gay when he was ten. It was the first time I saw him really breathe since Tom died. Really smile." She smiled too, confirming everything Aidan had ever known about her. Warm, loyal, accepting, she wanted whatever was best for her son, would accept him with open arms under any circumstances, same as she had her friends and Tom. It was a shame her family hadn't returned the favor.

"But then your family turned their backs on you," Jamie said, following his train of thought.

She nodded, then took another swallow before continuing. "We became tighter. The two of us were a unit. I had his back, and he had mine. But about a year ago, something changed. He said less, kept more to himself."

"Were there changes at school too? Who he hangs out with there?"

"He has a small group of friends, other queer kids like him, but now that you mention it, I began seeing less of them. But I was also working more." She fixed her gaze on the water bottle label as she cut through it with a nail. Her voice trembled when she spoke again. "I shouldn't have—"

Aidan covered her other hand. "Izzy, don't blame yourself. You were working to give him a future."

She continued to tear through the strip of paper but also didn't move her other hand out from under Aidan's. "I don't want what happened, what his dad did, what my family did, to ever hold him back."

"Any other changes in behavior?" Jamie asked.

"He stopped working on the truck."

Aidan's hand squeezed around hers. "The truck?"

"The one you found for Tom in La Honda."

"His Christmas present, before . . ."

She turned the hand under Aidan's over, clasping his back. "It was the only one of Tom's I didn't sell. It was the one worth the least . . ."

"Because it needed the most work."

"Figured it would keep Angel busy the longest."

There was a long moment of silence, a remembrance and a truce reached, before Izzy withdrew her hand. When she spoke again, some of the earlier chill had left her voice. "If you can help him, please do."

"Would it be okay if I talked to him?" Jamie asked. "I lost my dad when I was a little younger than him, and I know a thing or two about cars."

She stopped cutting through the paper. "You think he'll tell you what you need to know?"

"I think I'm a new face, someone he can relate to, and maybe that gets us more information that can help get him a deal."

She nodded. "Okay, thank you."

"I'd like to get a list of those friends too," Aidan said, then, anticipating her objection, added, "We won't question anyone without letting you know, but we can see if they intersect with the other people involved in the case."

"All right."

Standing, Jamie grabbed a pad of paper off the credenza and handed it to Izzy. She scribbled a short list, tore off the sheet, and handed it to Aidan.

"Hang tight," he said, rising next to Jamie. "Let us see what we can do."

He turned to leave, but Izzy's hand around his wrist stopped him. "Thank you. You didn't have to help—"

"Yeah, I did, Isabella. I made a promise the day he was born and the day he was christened. I should've never turned my back on that."

She gazed up at him with dark eyes, full of the same regret Aidan had been drowning in the past two days. "I didn't give you much choice."

"Gabe and Tom didn't give either of us any choice. But we have one now." He squeezed her hand. "We do what's best for Angel."

She squeezed back with a nod. "Thank you."

Aidan followed Jamie out the door, pulling it shut behind them, and found Rick waiting in the hallway. "I may have something," he said. "Or maybe someone. Beverly Kildare. She's a foster kid in the home of Darien White's sister and a student at Angel's school. Couple years behind him."

Aidan checked the list Izzy had given him. Not on there. But worth an ask. He opened the conference room door again. "Izzy?"

She looked up from her phone. "Yeah?"

"Does Angel know a Beverly Kildare?"

"Sure, that's Bev, his Spanish tutor."

Aidan couldn't stop his brow from lifting, and Izzy's answering laugh felt good. Like the laugh that Christmas Day when Aidan had hauled the rusted-out chassis of a '66 Chevy truck into their yard. "Boy can speak it, the Spanish you and I know, but ask him to write it for class, and it's a disaster."

"I'll make sure to ask him to write his statement in Spanish," he said with a wink before closing the door and turning back to Rick and Jamie. "Bev's his Spanish tutor."

"I'll see what else I can find on her," Rick said, already heading for the bullpen.

"This is good, Irish." Jamie smiled and squeezed his shoulder. "Now I've got more to work with. Let's go see what I can find out from Angel."

THIRTEEN

Jamie flashed his visitor's badge for the guard standing outside the interrogation room, the door partially open. "Jamie Walker, SAC Talley's husband. He asked me to wait with Angel."

The guard pushed the door the rest of the way open. "Let me know if you need anything."

"Will do, thanks." Jamie closed the door behind him, then leaned back against the wall, assessing the frowning young man on the other side of the table. In a dark suit, white shirt, and green and red striped tie, his curls tamed into submission, Angel looked ready to accompany his mom to Sunday Christmas service. A closer study, however, revealed bags under his eyes, torn-up cuticles, restless limbs, and a gnawed-on lower lip in serious need of balm. But the bitter huff that escaped his lips was all surly teen.

Jamie pushed off the wall and slid into the chair across from him. "Something funny?"

"How does he always get the hot ones?"

Jamie didn't have to ask who Angel was referring to.

"Have you seen him? He's pretty hot too." The hottest man Jamie had ever seen. Sure, he was biased where his husband was concerned, but he'd put Aidan up against anyone in a hotness contest.

Angel rolled his eyes. "The red hair is new."

"My doing." Jamie stretched a hand across the table. "Jamie Walker, Aidan's husband."

"I heard," Angel said as he shook his hand. Firmer than necessary, but Jamie let him have that. The kid was no doubt grasping for any straws of control within reach. "Angel Crane."

"I heard you have some questions about how I pulled that maneuver in the hipster wagon Saturday."

Angel's snicker was the reaction Jamie wanted. "I can't believe you pulled that off in that car."

"What else was I supposed to do with that giant ass-end?"

Snickering became laughter, then questions, which Jamie gamely answered. At some point, they would probably regret Jamie teaching him how to drift in any vehicle, but today, in this moment, it was the opening they needed, especially when Angel asked, "How'd you learn to drive like that?"

He rested his forearms on the table, leaning slightly forward in his chair. "My dad used to work on cars. I'd watch him like a hawk. He died when I was five, before I could get under the hood myself." Jamie didn't call attention to Angel's jolt or his widening eyes; just kept talking, kept offering connections. "My mom worked at a local diner. I'd hang out there after school, and there was a go-cart place next door. As soon as I was tall enough, I was behind the wheel, and if I tweaked a couple things on the engine that was right there in front of me . . ." He shrugged and rested back in his chair, legs crossed.

Angel tracked the movement, from Jamie's toe all the way to his head. "Guessin' you hit that 'this high' signpost early?"

"You could say that."

They shared another laugh, Angel's trailing off first. "I'm sorry about your dad," he said.

"I'm sorry about yours too." The silence that settled between them felt more comfortable than awkward. Jamie was getting somewhere with him, slowly but surely, and so, despite how much Jamie wanted to lean forward before delivering his next thought, he hung back, giving Angel space to react. "You know . . . what he did, he did to protect you and your family."

Angel quickly averted his gaze. "He left us."

"I didn't know him," Jamie said. "But from what Aidan's told me, I'm fairly certain that was never Tom's intention. Just like you'd never voluntarily leave Bev either."

Angel's gaze whipped back to his, and all those earlier signs of anxiety and exhaustion manifested in his wide blue eyes, along with a heaping side of fear.

Jamie did lean forward then. "We can help you, Angel. We can help Bev, whatever the situation."

He shook his head. "If I talk, they won't let her come back."

"To school?"

Angel didn't nod, just locked his desperate gaze with Jamie's. Then, after a seemingly endless few seconds, he blinked. Was he . . .

Jamie tested his theory. "Did White give you the briefcase?"

Another blink.

It was a razor-thin interpretation of "not talking" but a technicality Angel was smart enough to see and use. A way to communicate the help he needed because he and Aidan were right: Angel was protecting someone.

Beverly Kildare.

"Is White's sister, Deidra, working with him?"

A slower blink, and Angel dug his teeth into his lip so hard he winced.

"She doesn't want to be?" Jamie tried.

Two blinks—not quite right—and when Angel stared back at him, his bright blue eyes were watery, pity and anger swirling together in the glassy sheen.

"Or Deidra just doesn't care," Jamie guessed, his stomach sinking at the reality of a too common story. "As long as the state and White pay her."

Angel caved, unable to hold the emotions in any longer. "Get Bev out, please. I tried, I did what White wanted, both times, at the port and then taking that briefcase for him. He was supposed to get paid and leave. And once he paid Deidra, she'd go on a bender like she always does, and I could get Bev out of there. But I screwed up and got caught, and now I don't know what's happened to Bev."

"Hey, hey, hey." Jamie covered his hands that were splayed on the table. "You did good, Angel. Real good. We'll take it from here."

FOURTEEN

Jamie had already been in the field once on this case—with questionable authority. There'd been no one around on Saturday morning to argue with an SAC over whether his former-agent husband should be involved in a high-speed car chase. Matt and Rick knew him, vouched for him, and the other agents involved that morning were familiar with his reputation.

But today there was a man who indeed looked like a Rooster—a mane the color of hay, a dark suit so shiny it reminded Jamie of an oil slick, and words that were sharp as a bird's beak—who made it clear that whether Angel was charged with a felony or misdemeanor depended on White's arrest and that nothing, including a former-fed-now-civilian, would jeopardize the joint task-force take-down and the leverage they needed to make White talk.

And Aidan asked Jamie to stay with Angel and Izzy.

Jamie didn't argue. Instead, he drove his precious cargo by their home so they could grab clean clothes and toiletries, then took them to the condo he and Aidan were borrowing, all under guard. Once inside, Jamie insisted mother and son catch up on much-needed sleep while he caught up on game tape from the tourney. Which he did for a while, then anticipating it could be a long day and night of waiting, he started a batch of chili in the crock pot and modeled a '66 Chevy C10 on his tablet. He also hunted down every handbook and manual he could find on the beast and called the best mechanic he knew in San Francisco to chat engines and other modifications. He'd just hung up with her when Angel shuffled down the stairs.

Jamie wrinkled his nose at the kid's attire—Lakers sweats and a Dodgers T-shirt. "All of that is wrong."

Following his nose, Angel snooped around the crock pot in the kitchen. "Well, I'm not wearing Warriors *or* Giants shi —stuff."

Jamie pretended to be outraged. "You're from San Francisco!"

"I won't tell you about the Raiders gear I left at home."

Continuing his dramatics, Jamie closed his tablet, pushed it aside, then hid his head under his arms on the table, groaning, "Make it stop."

Angel's chuckle was a welcome sound, as was his "smells good" as he filled a glass with water. His shoulders were still higher than Jamie liked to see on a young person, but this Angel was a much different kid from the surly, anxiety-stricken one of the past few days.

"Slow cooker chili," Jamie said as he rose. "Perfect winter food." He cruised along the other side of the island to the fridge for eggs and milk, then to the pantry for a pan and box of cornbread mix, before he claimed the stool by the mixing bowl he'd set out. "How's your mom?"

"Asleep still. She's always out for a while after the long ones."

"And she flew three of them in a row."

Angel hung his head and rubbed a hand over his nape. "Don't remind me."

"She's a parent," Jamie said as he cracked an egg into the bowl. "She did what she had to do."

"Because I screwed up."

"You were a friend doing what you had to. Tell me about her, Bev."

"She's gorgeous."

Jamie stopped midstir and raised a brow. Maybe Angel was bi instead of gay, like he'd told his mother.

"Not my type," he continued as he climbed onto a stool. "At least not that way. And I'm not hers either. She's ace."

"Your mom said she's your Spanish tutor?"

"Yeah, she's smart as hell, but most of the idiots at school don't see past her looks. The girls pull their mean girl act since all the guys hit on her, even though she's got zero interest in any of them. But she's the last person to fight back or speak up for herself."

"'Cause she's a foster kid." Jamie had seen it before, especially in his volunteer work. "So you pulled her into the queer kids club?"

Angel nodded.

"How'd you get her to do that?" Jamie asked as he poured the cornbread batter into the pan.

"Told her I didn't need a gringo to teach me Spanish."

Jamie laughed. "You didn't?"

"She was determined to prove me wrong." Smiling, his gaze drifted out the window, lost in a pleasant memory. "I had my test paper in my hand that day. Got a D. She snatched it from me, found three more errors the teacher missed, and changed the D to an F." He shook his head, laughing. "Big yikes."

"But you also found your best friend."

"Bet," he replied with a lift of his chin, before his gaze snagged on Jamie's emerald-inlaid wedding ring. "Tell me about him, other than how you got him to dye his hair red."

"Back red," Jamie corrected as he rested against the counter by the stove. "That's his natural color."

"Figured." Angel rolled his glass between his palms, seeming to drift through another memory. "I went to a couple birthday parties back in the day. All the Talley kids around then were redheaded."

"There's a whole army now, and Aidan is everyone's favorite uncle."

"You two got kids?"

"Not yet, but we're starting to make plans for them." While he and Aidan had paused the conversation owing to the kid in front of him, Jamie would pick it back up when the time was right. He wasn't going to let this speed bump slow them down in the long run, not when they were finally starting to pick up speed.

"He'll make a good father."

Jamie and Angel jerked their gazes to the stairs, the direction the comment had come from. Izzy was making her way down in similarly casual clothing, though thankfully not in more dreadfully offensive sportswear.

She climbed onto the stool beside Angel and bumped his shoulder. "He doted on you and Katie," she said, then aimed a soft, genuinely concerned look at Jamie. "Is he really okay?"

"He wasn't," Jamie told them. "Not for a while. For

eight months, no one believed him that Gabe and Tom were murdered. He thought he was losing his mind, but he knew it here." He laid a hand over his chest. "He also knew he was supposed to die in that crash too. That guilt will always be there, that he walked away with only nightmares and pins in his arm, but he tries to survive for them."

Izzy cast her gaze aside, swallowing hard. "I'm glad he has you."

"I'm the lucky one." Had been since the day Mel had assigned him to be Aidan's new partner. Was even luckier that Aidan had taken him back after the secrets Jamie had kept. Was luckiest of all that Aidan had taken another chance on love and forever with him. "We're all lucky to still have him."

She swiped away a tear that raced down her cheek, and Angel circled her shoulders, holding her tight to him, the unit she'd spoken of earlier, each of them having the other's back.

It was a quiet moment, a good healing one that he sensed they needed, and he hated that the beeping slow cooker interrupted it. The interruption that came a minute later, though, was much more welcome. Withdrawing his vibrating phone from his pocket, Jamie read the incoming text from Aidan and smiled. "Aidan's back. They just pulled into the parking garage downstairs."

"They?" Angel said, more hope and joy in that one word than Jamie had yet to hear in the teen's voice.

"With Bev."

Angel was off the stool and out the door before Izzy could holler, "Angel, wait!"

"Go," Jamie said to her. "Stairs are to the left. I'm right behind you." He flicked off the oven, then sprinted out the door behind them, emerging on the ground floor in time to see Angel and Bev collide mid–parking lot, arms around each other, laughing. Jamie looked past the two friends, to his husband whose autumn eyes shone with happiness and relief, and in that moment, Jamie had never been more proud to be Aidan Talley's husband.

FIFTEEN

Aidan was soaking in the oversize tub when Jamie entered the dimly lit bathroom. "Everything good out there?"

"I modeled the Chevy on my tablet," Jamie said as he stripped off his T-shirt and jeans, his athletic grace never ceasing to amaze him. All those long limbs and he rarely got caught in his clothes like Aidan often did. Often got caught in Jamie's too, his husband leaving them strewn everywhere. "Also downloaded all the manuals I could find and called Celia for a list of potential modifications. Should keep him busy." He tapped Aidan's shoulder, and Aidan scooted forward, making room for Jamie to sink in behind him. "And he's got his best friend back." He wrapped himself around Aidan, arms over his torso and calves over his shins. "You did good out there today."

The tight hold buttressed Aidan against the shudder-inducing memory of what they'd found at Deidra's place.

"You want to talk about it?" Jamie asked.

The instinct was there to close his eyes and hide, but that would only bring the mental replay into sharper focus

—dirty dishes piled on every surface, trash cans overflowing with food wrappers and takeout boxes, soiled clothes in a pile by the laundry room, and ashtrays full of cigarette butts. Flies in the stale nicotine-tinged air and a rat scurrying out of the kitchen and down the short hall toward where they'd found Bev camped out in a closet, the only neat and clean place in the entire house.

Aidan focused instead on his husband's hands splayed across his chest, Jamie's knuckles knobby from the hacking and basketball, the band on his left ring finger safely in place, just like Jamie kept him. "We hear stories when we're working cases with fosters or when we interact with the kids at the Madigan shelters. I knew here"—he tapped his temple—"what some foster kids go through, but actually seeing it . . ." He scooted back against Jamie, trying and failing to disappear into him. "I was lucky to have the family I did."

"So was I," Jamie said. "So is Angel."

Crossing his arms, he clasped Jamie's biceps around him. "You did good today too, getting Angel more comfortable and talking."

"He's a good kid. He was just trying to do what was right to help his friend. Kind of like his dad."

The thought had swirled around in the back of Aidan's head all day, ever since they'd discovered Beverly Kildare and Angel's connection to her. Tom had done the wrong thing too, but he'd done it to help Isabella's grandmother, to protect his family. Did Aidan wish Tom—and Gabe, for that matter—had gone about things differently? Yes. Could he continue to hold on to those last vestiges of hurt and blame that occasionally haunted him? He'd forgiven Gabe, but not Tom, and maybe that was part of the reason he'd let

Isabella push him away too, the pain of betrayal from the man who'd sworn to have his back still too fresh. Holding on to it still wasn't going to bring Izzy and Angel back into his life. And he wanted that; no question after the last few days.

With a long, slow breath, Aidan let the ghosts go, once and for all.

Behind him, Jamie chuckled. "How long have you needed to do that?"

"Too long." He rested his head back on Jamie's shoulder, breathing with him and letting the warmth chase away the day's chills. Letting each swipe of the washcloth Jamie made over his skin relax him further.

He couldn't say how much time had passed when Jamie spoke again. "How long do we have Bev for?"

Aidan smiled, liking the way that sounded. For the time being, he and Jamie could give her a safe, clean place to stay, which Aidan suspected she hadn't had for some time. "She's technically a witness in protective custody. Rooster will want to question her. Maybe she overheard something, like who White is working for or who Angel was supposed to deliver those diamonds to. She didn't mention either in her initial statement, but we didn't dig too deep. It was more about the immediate circumstances."

"Understandably. I'll help finalize the protective custody paperwork tomorrow."

"I'm hoping Rick has it filled out by the time we get in." He lifted his hands, fingers spread wide. "Jazz Hands for the win."

Laughing, Jamie laced their fingers together and crossed their arms back over Aidan's chest. "What about social services?"

"I'm sure they'll be by the office tomorrow."

"Do you think they'll place her back with Deidra?"

"They better never place another kid with that person. She was harboring a felon who'd violated parole, and the condition of that place . . ." He shook his head, dislodging the visions. "We took pictures. Plenty of documentation."

"You brought them both in?"

He nodded. "Matt took White to holding. Berat took the sister to County."

"Good," Jamie said as he lazily brushed their joined hands over his torso, lulling Aidan back into the jelly-limbed place. "Izzy has a flight tomorrow. She's trying to get out of it, but they're short-staffed and the pay is double."

"The kids can stay here." There was a delay between the words that had come out of his mouth and the presumptions that belatedly registered in his brain. Once they did, Aidan rotated half around in Jamie's arms, hand over the tattoo on his chest, the place it automatically went to after years together. "If that's okay with you? We have the place for the week, right?"

"We do," he said, covering Aidan's hand and giving it a squeeze. And if that wasn't reassurance enough, the soft kiss he laid on Aidan's lips quieted his spike of overstepping anxiety. "I was hoping you'd say that, though I think it would be good for both of them to get back to school tomorrow, assuming Rooster agrees. Under guard, of course."

"Agreed." Aidan settled his weight on Jamie's chest and smiled against his lips. "Is this what it would be like?"

"Soon, I hope," Jamie said with a grin, clearly following his train of thought. "Though if our future involves spending more time with Izzy and Angel, we gotta get 'em back to the Bay Area. I can't with the Lakers and Dodgers fans here."

"Not to mention the true-blue UCLA of it all."

Jamie lunged, splashing water. "Shut your filthy mouth." He proceeded to do just that, swallowing Aidan's laughter as their lips met again, then his moans as their kisses grew more heated. Ratcheted hotter when Jamie reached beneath the water and palmed Aidan's sac, stiffening his half-hard cock the rest of the way to erect. "Maybe we should practice that whole having to be quiet thing."

"We should," Aidan said. "Because after seven years, we both know you're pretty fucking terrible at it."

"Me?" Jamie squawked, proving his point, and Aidan shifted again, the one to silence him this time. He captured Jamie's lips and aligned their cocks, taking them both in hand and stroking. Jamie groaned against his lips. "Fuck, Irish." He rolled his hips, all of that big, gorgeous body grinding up against Aidan's. Hungry, same as Aidan was for him, for the comfort and peace only Jamie could give him.

"I know, baby, I know," he whispered as he pumped them faster, the water sloshing, waves that mimicked the heat rushing in Aidan's veins. He braced himself with his free hand against the side of the tub behind Jamie's head, getting more leverage and a good look at his whole world straining with pleasure beneath him. Head thrown back, Jamie panted and bit back his moans, his chest heaving, his nails digging into Aidan's sides to urge him faster. Harder. Could Aidan ask for more than this perfection? He wanted to. "Can we do this, Whiskey? Can we have it all?"

Jamie locked his lust-darkened gaze on his. "We can do anything, Irish. Together."

Which was how they came, erupting over Aidan's fist and swallowing each other's moans.

Quiet.

Proof they could do this much.

And with Jamie by his side, Aidan was hopeful about the rest too. Was starting to believe that yes, maybe they could have it all.

SIXTEEN

Aidan beat Jamie out of the bedroom the next morning, determined to take care of him—or at least his coffee—as a thank-you for looking after him the past few days. He wasn't surprised to find Bev and Angel still in the living room, the former asleep on the oversize couch, the latter passed out on his folded arms at the nearby table. Jamie's tablet had been pushed to the side, no doubt so Angel could keep Bev in his sights as he'd fallen asleep. He was a good kid, a protector like his dad had been, and for the first time in six long years, thoughts of Tom didn't come with anger, only wisps of sadness that his former friend wasn't here to see the man his son was growing up to be.

Approaching the table, Aidan whisper-shouted a "Hey, Angel." When that didn't wake him, he gently shook his godson's shoulder.

Angel reacted instantly, surging out of his chair and swinging like a bat out of hell, acting on pure instinct. Aidan had those too, Bureau honed, plus several inches and a lot more weight on Angel too. Catching one of Angel's wrists on the way to spinning behind him, he stretched Angel's arm across his front. Confused, Angel flailed with his other arm, which Aidan also caught and crossed over the other, effectively pinning his arms to his chest and his back to Aidan's front. A gentle but firm hold. "Angel, it's me, it's Aidan," he said, speaking with his full accent, aiming to startle Angel's waking brain back to reality. "You're safe. I'm not a threat."

After another few seconds of struggling, something must have clicked, Angel stilling in his arms. "Aidan?"

"Yeah, it's me."

Tension rushed out of his lanky frame. "Fuck, man, I'm sorry."

Aidan released his wrists and circled around to Angel's front, keeping a steadying hand on his shoulder. "Where'd you learn to do that?"

He sank back into his seat. "The Internet."

"Of course."

"Don't knock it 'cause you're old."

Crisis averted, snark back in effect, Aidan continued on his intended trajectory to the kitchen. "I'll have you know, I learned to truss a turkey from the Internet."

"You're like fifty, aren't you? How did you not know that?"

"Forty-nine," he corrected as he replaced yesterday's grounds with fresh ones. "For a few more months, at least, and as for the trussing, Jamie's the chef. I can cook a few things well, mostly Latin food and Irish staples, but there was this year when Jamie was on the road with the team right up until Thanksgiving morning, and I was determined to have the turkey ready when he got home."

"How'd that go?"

He pressed the Brew button, then rested back against the counter. "Paid the neighbor an *obscene* amount of money for theirs."

Angel laughed, then, catching sight of his still sleeping friend, slapped a hand over his mouth to stifle the sound.

"You didn't have to stay up," Aidan said. "There's a guard outside."

"I know, I just—"

"I get it. Jamie was hurt pretty badly once. I stayed by his bedside all night, even with Mel and Danny right outside and all of us in a CIA safe house."

Angel's eyes grew wide. "What—"

"Nope, above your pay grade," he said as he turned back to the coffee pot. "How do you take your coffee?" He probably should have asked Izzy if Angel was allowed to have coffee at all, but if he was anything like his mother, he'd been drinking the stuff half his life already.

"Little bit of coffee in my milk and cinnamon. Please."

Aidan smiled. Just like his mother, who had left before dawn for an up-and-back to Seattle. Izzy had also agreed with Jamie's suggestion from last night. "Are y'all up for school today?"

Angel scoffed. "Y'all?"

"It slips sometimes." Aidan brought Angel's coffee and cinnamon milk to the table. "Hazards of being married to a Southerner. We'll get you and Bev there, then Ward will bring you to the office afterward."

"The guard? He's gonna be on us all day? He's huge, everyone will—"

"He knows how to hang back. He's used to protecting rock stars."

"For real? What rock stars do you know?"

"Not me, but friends." Both Matt and Levi had connections to the LA music scene, and Ward had come highly recommended. "The federal prosecutor may have more questions for Bev, and I'm sure he'll have some for you too."

Angel sipped his coffee, quiet for a moment before speaking again, his voice sincere, void of its usual snark and with a hefty dose of regret. "I'm sorry I didn't cooperate. I just didn't want them to hurt her. Maybe if I'd said something sooner . . ."

Aidan lowered into the chair beside him. "Don't play that game with yourself. She's here now. She's safe." He covered Angel's hand with his. "And so are you."

Angel lifted his hopeful blue gaze to Aidan's. "I'm starting to believe you."

SEVENTEEN

"Everything look good?" Jamie asked Matt, who'd agreed to give the protective custody paperwork a final once-over.

Rick had given them a massive head start, completing the bulk of it before Jamie and Aidan had arrived. They'd just needed to fill in some details, and once done, there was no one better to check over the final package than Matt. Prior to moving out west, he'd worked with Cam on kidnap and rescue cases in Boston. Much of their caseload had involved working with juvenile victims and witnesses; he'd seen plenty of these forms over his career.

"I know you've filled these out before," Matt said as he skimmed the pages. "Cam told me about that child pornography case he worked with you and Aidan early on. You had to place all those kids afterward."

Jamie shivered, remembering that bone- and soul-chilling bust on a foggy September morning. Matt was right; they'd had to arrange protective custody for dozens of kids pending conclusion of the case. But that custody paperwork and the paperwork for this case were fundamentally different, at least where it concerned him and Aidan. "We didn't place any of those kids with us."

"So, why's Bev different? We have usual channels for this. Safe houses and fosters that have been vetted."

"Because she's important to Angel." He glanced past Matt, Aidan's red hair catching his attention as he and Berat led a handcuffed White to the interrogation room. "And because Angel is important to Aidan. He can't—won't—disappoint him again."

Matt handed the paperwork back to him. "It's perfect, but you knew that already."

"Another pair of eyes never hurts."

"Fair," Matt said, then tilted his head toward the interrogation room. "So come with me to observe in case I miss something, at least until social services gets here."

Jamie neatened up the stack of papers, then followed Matt. "You think this case is related to your jewel thief one?"

"On the front end, I doubt it," Matt said as he closed the observation room door behind them. "The thefts I've been looking into are clean, neat, professional. But I'm not ruling out that the end buyer could be the same." He flicked on the speaker so they could hear what was said on the other side of the one-way glass.

As Berat went over identification particulars with White and his public defender across the table, Jamie studied their suspect. Late thirties, white, greasy brown hair, sunken brown eyes, dingy clothes that hung loose on his thin frame. Meth head, Jamie recalled from White's rap sheet, and by the sweat dotting his brow and his bouncing knee beneath the table, withdrawal was starting to kick in.

Potentially good for their team.

"Tell us what you were doing at Long Beach Port on Friday," Aidan said from beside Berat.

"I wasn't there," White replied.

Berat opened a file folder and withdrew a picture. He pushed it across the table in front of White. "That's you behind the wheel of a truck we found off the 125 in San Diego County. Sounds to me like you were violating parole."

"You found me here. I didn't violate my parole."

"But you were in that truck."

"Okay, fine, yeah, that's me." He flicked a dismissive hand at the picture. "I was filling in for a friend. He couldn't make it to the port on time, so I picked up his load." His jittery gaze bounced around the room, and his knee bounced faster with each lie he added to the pile. "I met him in Torrance. That's still LA County."

"And the opposite direction of San Diego," Aidan said.

White shrugged. "Not my business where he went with it afterward."

"What's this friend's name?" Berat asked.

"Peter."

"Peter who?"

"I don't know."

"Because there was no Peter." Aidan rested his forearms on the table, leaning forward. "You drove the truck to El Segundo Beach, where you gave a briefcase of stolen goods to Angel Crane."

White slumped in his chair, away from Aidan. Whether he realized it or not, White was telegraphing that every word out of his mouth was bullshit. That Aidan and company were dangerously close to the truth. Jamie wondered if that was why the PD remained silent; he already knew this was an open-and-shut case, at least against White.

Who continued to dig his hole deeper. "That kid's full of shit."

Berat slid another sheet of paper across the table. "Your fingerprints are all over the windowsill of the car he was driving."

"Yeah, cause he's all the time visiting my sister's ward. The two of 'em are attached at the hip, always talking in not American so we can't understand."

Jamie rolled his eyes. "Who wants to tell him American isn't a language?"

Inside the room, Rooster spoke for the first time, his voice carefully neutral. "Her ward?"

White's gaze shot to Rooster leaning against the wall, and some of his jitteriness calmed. Sensing an ally, Jamie supposed, in the man who looked and sounded the most like him in the room. "Yeah," he said, a half-smile exposing his stained teeth. "Deidra lets her stay. Puts a roof over her head."

"And that's about all," Matt remarked beside Jamie.

"State don't give her nearly enough for it."

"So you do," Rooster said. "With the money you make from selling meth."

White deflated, the smile slipping from his face.

"Here's the problem, Darien," Aidan said, drawing the criminal's attention back to him. "Your prints are *also* all over the stolen tags *you* put on Angel's car. You weren't filling in for someone. *You* hijacked that truck out from under another driver's nose. We have his statement."

Jamie didn't think it was possible for White's skin to

blanch more, but as Aidan continued, he continued to edge toward ghostly.

"You coerced Angel into being your accomplice by having your sister hold his friend hostage so he'd show up at the port and help you steal that truck. Then, you had him ferry the stolen goods to another party for you."

"We don't care about a meth head," Rooster said. "You're not worth my time to prosecute. Rate you're going, you'll overdose or cross the wrong person soon enough."

He gulped, audibly enough for Jamie to hear through the speaker.

"Or maybe you already did," Rooster said. "That's the person we want."

"Did you know what you were transporting?" Berat asked.

"You don't have to answer that," White's PD said.

He glanced his direction. "But I got nothin' to hide. I didn't know." He turned back to Berat. "It was just a briefcase."

"The value of its contents put you squarely in grand theft territory."

Rooster hummed. "Maybe I'll rethink that prosecution."

White mumbled a curse and skated a shaking hand through his hair.

"Doing the math, Darien?" Aidan said. "With your record, that's three strikes. Twenty-five years in prison. I wonder how many people in there you've crossed."

Too many, apparently. Tipping point reached, White lurched forward, beseeching. "Okay, look, I got upside down on some stuff. I owe money to this guy, Pudge."

"Pudge?"

"Patrick something, skinny, freckled fucker. He runs

stuff, I don't know for who. He said I do this one run, and my debts would be clear."

"And you were too much of a chickenshit to do it yourself."

"Look, I needed a hit, but I needed to get clear too."

"That's why you called Angel back in?" Aidan's voice vibrated with anger. "Because you got fucked up?"

"He did good at the port, distracting folks like I told him, and I knew he'd do it again. Anything for that girl." He rolled his eyes and puffed out his chest, sneering. "Sorry excuse for a faggot."

On the other side of the glass, Berat's arm flung in front of Aidan was the only reason Aidan didn't get his hands around White's neck, while on Jamie's side, Matt's arm around his middle was the only thing keeping Jamie from barreling through the door to his husband.

White tried to push his chair back, away from the immediate threat, and missed the one he'd thought friendly before. Quicker than Jamie could blink away the red in his own gaze, Rooster was beside the table, a foot hooked around the leg of White's chair, foiling his escape.

"Did you know who Angel was delivering that briefcase to?" Rooster demanded. "All you told him was a white guy in a black Benz on the third floor of the P-7 at LAX." When White didn't answer, Rooster leaned closer, a shark's grin curling one corner of his mouth. "You know, maybe I will prosecute you. For attempted murder."

"How do you get that?" White protested.

Rooster grabbed the front of his shirt and hauled him nose to nose. Every word he bit out was full of the same anger that had colored Aidan's voice earlier. "Because *you* sent a kid to a meet not knowing a name, with only half the information he needed to survive it. What stops mister mysterious from just ending him right there? Making your and your sister's lives a hell of a lot easier. You get your money and keep collecting from the state. Sounds premeditated to me. And with that silly snake tattoo on your arm, I'm sure I can sell it to a jury. One less brown faggot in your lily-white world." He shoved White back in his chair, hard enough to make it wobble on two legs. "I don't take kindly to assholes who set kids up. Especially ones like me."

White brought the chair down, barely, and darted a gaze at Aidan and Berat. "Are you just going to let him threaten me like that? You're cops. He can't do that."

"My husband's in the other room," Aidan said.

"And I'm brown too," Berat said, waving a hand in front of his face. "Also very gay."

White took up knee bouncing again, the speed increasing as Rooster propped a hip on the table and crossed his arms over his puffed-out chest, a much more intimidating display than White's earlier. "News flash, despite what your cult leads you to believe, us queer folk are in the criminal justice and law enforcement systems, and just your luck, you got them all on your case. You're outnumbered, you racist, homophobic junkie, so start talking."

White glanced at his PD, who remained as quiet as he had throughout the interrogation. Finding no help, he finally folded. "Fine. Pudge told me his name was Arty. Arty Martino."

"Shit," Jamie cursed.

"You know him?" Matty asked.

"Arthur Martino was a mob fence Aidan and Tom put

away a decade ago." He remembered Arty's name from the case file index he'd reviewed again yesterday.

Judging by Aidan's stiff frame, he'd made the connection too. But before Jamie could tap on the window or open the door to confirm, Aidan's phone vibrated in his pocket. He pulled it out, an incoming call from Danny lighting up the screen. "Danny, it's Jamie," he answered. "Aidan's right in the middle—"

"There's been another theft," Danny said, cutting him off. "And this one's on us."

EIGHTEEN

Aidan swung the Outback into the same spot in the Talley's LB port yard that he'd occupied on Friday, except today Matt and Berat were in the car behind his and Jamie's, and waiting for them in front of the office was KJ Harman, Talley Enterprises' new chief of security. They'd been on the phone with KJ off and on this past weekend, bringing her up to speed. Now, Aidan needed her to return the favor. "Catch us up," he said as they joined her.

"Electronic goods didn't make it where they were supposed to go."

She handed him a manifest, and Aidan flipped through the multipage document. This wasn't a small cargo truck with two pallets and a briefcase of diamonds. This was a jam-packed eighteen-wheeler worth of phones, televisions, computers, and other electronic goods. Less overall value than Parsons's shipment, but the sort of haul Talley Enterprises handled every day. The fact it had gone missing could end up being more damaging to the company's reputation than the Parsons theft.

"Anything off with the pickup?" Berat asked.

She handed him a separate stack of papers. "Driver had the correct paperwork and everything."

Jamie peered over his shoulder. "Forgeries?"

"Not exactly. Standard operating procedure is to check paper orders against the ones submitted online. Everything matched."

Which meant someone had hacked their system and uploaded fake papers. Another problem that opened TE up to future thefts. Thankfully, Aidan and TE had a top-notch hacker in the family. "Jamie—"

"I'm on it," he said, already halfway up the steps to the office door.

Avoiding the frosted garland that had been added to the exterior over the weekend, KJ rested against the raised cement foundation that formed flower beds around the modular office unit. "Two thefts in five days." She gathered her thick fall of blond waves into a bun and shed her suit jacket, December in LA a good deal warmer than in the Bay Area. "More than we've had in five years."

"Related?" Aidan asked Matt and Berat. They had more experience than him in cargo theft matters—and in Los Angeles.

"Fifty-fifty shot," Berat answered. "The prior theft was a specific high-value item. Yes, someone off-loaded the rest of the goods eventually, but they were after the diamonds first and foremost."

"But they didn't go about it like a professional crew," Matt said. "Not like the thieves I've been investigating. For years. And I've gotten nowhere. One weekend and we've already got a suspect in custody."

"The incident today," Berat said, "falls somewhere in the

middle. More like Matt's case in that it's organized. Fake papers, planning, etcetera. Less like it in that we're talking run-of-the-mill cargo theft of consumer goods."

"The run-of-the-mill sort is rampant," KJ said. "At ports, at truck stops, at delivery depots. Ever since the pandemic." Her phone rang, and she excused herself around the corner to take the call.

"Do you think anything about the guy with the truck-load of oranges on the corner?" Berat said to Aidan.

"Or the computer parts you can buy on you-name-it online platform?" Matt added. "Other than the fact they're cheaper than at the name-brand store? Cargo theft is also a favorite of organized crime these days. Easy money, relatively."

"With multiple ports here," Berat said, "it's a significant part of LAPD's and LBPD's caseloads."

Aidan considered the various players and facts, trying to tie them together. "Do we think the diamond theft could have also been organized crime? When Tom and I put Arty away, he'd been working for the mob. And we know White was dealing meth and in hock to this Pudge guy. We need to pull together a list of crews that run cargo thefts and drugs. Mafia, Bratva, Triad, the cartels, check them all."

Matt lifted his phone. "I'll give Charlie a call." Charlotte Henby was a friend of the family—one of her husbands was tight with Marsh—and an agent with the Bureau's organized crime unit.

Matt had barely stepped away when Jamie stepped out of the office.

"Any luck?" Aidan asked.

"Someone knew what they were doing."

"Can you track them?"

"Of course."

Aidan grinned at the familiar response until Jamie glanced at the phone in his hand and his smile waned.

"Danny?" Aidan guessed.

Jamie shook his head. "Double whammy," he answered. "Ward texted that the kids just ditched class. And according to Rooster, social services will be at the office in an hour."

NINETEEN

"This is the last place I expected them to come back to," Aidan said as Berat swung his cruiser onto Deidra White's street.

Sure enough, a familiar black Charger was parked in the driveway of the third house down, and at the curb across the street, Ward stood leaning against the side of his truck.

"You said the kid usually has a good reason for what he does." Berat parked behind the truck. "That's why you didn't have Ward bring them in. Let's see what plays out here."

He pushed open his car door, and Aidan followed, the two of them joining Ward by his truck. "I told them they couldn't lose you," Aidan said.

"Amateurs." Ward's smirk reached all the way to his light green eyes. "You wouldn't believe the shit rock stars try to pull."

"I don't want to know," Aidan said with a laugh before turning his attention toward the house. "How long have they been in there?"

"About twenty minutes."

"Anyone else?"

Ward shook his head. "When I realized they were headed here, I beat them to it. Looked around. It's just the two of 'em."

Aidan asked Ward to keep watch, then crossed the street with Berat. "Mind if I go in alone?" Aidan asked as they navigated the crumbling pavers that led to the rickety front porch.

"Go for it," Berat said. "I wanted to look around more out here. See if we missed anything the other day."

He disappeared around the side, and Aidan entered through the unlocked front door. "Angel!" he called. "Bev!"

Two *thunks* echoed from somewhere down the hallway, followed by "Shit" in Angel's voice, then "Tonto del culo" in Bev's.

Aidan laughed, then immediately regretted it, the action causing him to inhale more of the stale, awful odors that had intensified over the past twenty-four hours. "Please tell me you came back here for a good reason."

His godson poked his head into the hallway. "How'd you find us?"

Aidan tipped his head toward the street.

Angel stepped to the end of the hallway and glanced out the front window—at Ward by the curb where Aidan had left him. Angel straightened with a sigh. "I thought we'd lost him."

"You can't." Aidan shoved his hands in his pockets and moved to lean his shoulder against a wall, then thought better of it and stayed in relatively unsoiled territory. "Now," he said, voice neutral, keeping the objective in mind, "give me a good reason we're here."

"You're not mad?" Bev appeared at Angel's side, her blond hair gathered in a messy, wobbly bun. She had a pair of lab goggles hanging around her neck—and was that a piece of insulation on her shoulder?

Aidan grew even more intrigued. "I'm not happy," he said, "but I didn't put a guard on you only for your protection."

Bev elbowed her friend's side and muttered in Spanish, "Seems he knows you better than you think."

"Or," Aidan said, also in Spanish, "I just have enough teens and preteens in my life to know better."

"His Spanish is better than yours," Bev said to Angel, who elbowed her right back.

Aidan smiled at their antics. The resiliency of kids was a wonder. Angel had survived several hellish days, Bev countless more, and they were here today joking with each other, firmly in each other's corners.

"So, seriously," Aidan said, back to English. "Why are we here?"

Bev removed the goggles and lowered her chin, all of her earlier moxie vanishing. "My social worker called. Cara talked to Deidra and thinks 'we can make it work.'"

"I'm not gonna let that happen," Angel said.

Bev leaned her head on his shoulder and batted her lashes up at him. "My savior," she teased, though by the way her arm wound around his, holding tight, there was some truth to her words. But Bev, who, according to her file, had been a foster kid since she was eight, was also wise to reality. "I appreciate that you think you have a say. But you don't." She lifted her head and turned her attention back to Aidan. "I'm also tired of being the damsel in this scenario. Not my style." As if the shredded jeans, rock tee, and battered camo jacket didn't give it away. "Yeah, this sucked." She gestured around the house and wrinkled her nose, the freckles across the bridge melding together. "A lot. And I do not want to be back here. Ever. But while I was here, I kept my eyes and ears open. I thought I could help."

"One," Aidan said, "we're getting you out of here. I've worked this job long enough and made enough connections to make sure that happens." He stepped forward and crouched in front of her, making Beverly slightly taller than him, giving her the power that life and the system had taken from her. "In the meantime, you're welcome to stay with me and Jamie in protective custody. But it's your call, completely."

"Can Angel stay too?" Tone neutral, she asked the question casually, as if it were no big deal, but the way she shifted on her feet, the fact she didn't look away from Aidan, indicated it was in fact a *very* big deal. He guessed she rarely asked for any favors—and this one was non-negotiable.

"That's his and Izzy's call," he answered. "But as far as I'm concerned, you're both in protective custody while this case is ongoing. You're all welcome at the condo." He pointed at Angel's Dodgers hoodie as he rose. "Though Jamie's getting twitchy about the LA sports gear."

"They're good people," Angel said to Bev. "Except that part." Then to Aidan, "And my answer is yes, assuming Mom says it's okay."

Aidan bit back the smile that wanted to stretch across his face, keeping it as measured and professional as his heart could stand. "Okay, now that that's settled, can we talk outside about whatever you saw and heard? The smell in here is about to do me in."

"Need to show you a couple things first," Bev said as she turned on her heel, leading them back to the home's single bathroom at the end of the hallway. Despite the over tub window being open, the stench of mold and mildew made Aidan want to hurl, but seeing as Bev was climbing up onto the toilet lid, he had no choice but to hold it in. She lifted the picture off the wall above the toilet and handed it to Angel, then pointed at the writing on the wall. "Those are Darien's dealers and clients. I caught him scratching another name on here the other day."

Aidan squeezed into the narrow space on her left, between the toilet and sink, and skimmed the list of names, looking for anyone familiar. No one off the top of his—Wait. "Isn't your social worker's last name Dixon?"

"Yep," she said, popping the *p* like Angel had done the other night. She tapped the fifth name down with her blunt nail. "That's her brother."

"You are definitely not coming back here," Aidan said as he snapped pictures. "This is super helpful, Bev. Good job."

She preened as she rehung the picture, but once she hopped back down on the floor, some of her confidence diminished. "I should have pointed it out last night or taken a picture, but everything was . . ." She waved a hand in the air, as if that could summon the words.

"Moving pretty fast all of a sudden," Aidan completed for her. "And your job is to be a kid, not a detective."

"Okay, but, one more thing." She snapped her goggles back on and headed into the room she'd shared with Deidra's and Darien's junk, her space limited to the closet she'd kept in tip-top shape, a sharp contrast to the rest of the house. A step ladder was unfolded under a rectangular cutout in the closet ceiling, the heavy piece of wood that constituted a cover over it pushed slightly aside. It was the same sort of attic access as in the guest room closet of the home Aidan used to own before he'd move in with Jamie. "I hid up here once," Bev said as she climbed the ladder. "Before I realized the dust and insulation would kill my eyes. When Angel told me Darien got busted for smuggling stolen stuff, I thought about it again."

"That's what I was trying to open wider when you got here," Angel said, gesturing to the narrow attic opening Bev had slid through.

Wishing like hell he had his own pair of goggles and saying a prayer for the contents of his stomach, Aidan climbed the ladder. Reaching the opening, he pushed the cover the rest of the way aside and hefted himself up. On his knees, not enough clearance to stand, Aidan took one look around and covered his mouth with his hand. In part to keep out the dust and insulation, in part to cover his gaping surprise. "Hey, Angel," he called from behind his fingers. "Can you ask Berat—"

A section of the attic's back slatted wall swung open—a hidden door beneath the structure's A-frame. Blinding light streamed in, dust streamed out, then a blink later, Berat's face and shoulders appeared at the opening. "Ask me what —" Berat started before gaping too. "I noticed this section of the siding didn't line up. Guess I know why now."

Aidan glanced again at the boxes of electronics and other electronic goods stacked at one end of the attic from floor to ceiling. "I think it's safe to say the two thefts are connected."

TWENTY

Jamie was practiced at maintaining his Southern charm in hostile situations. He'd learned as a player and coach and as a federal agent that his smile and accent tended to get him further faster than bluster and fury. When he and Aidan had been partnered, he was usually the polite cop to Aidan's surly one. But when Cara Dixon, Beverly's social worker, suggested that Bev be placed back in Deidra White's care, Jamie's genteel manner took a flying leap out the window. "Explain to us why you think it's a good idea to put Bev back in that house?" he practically growled.

Even Matt's neutral agent mode broke, anger coloring his cheeks. "She was hiding in a closet when we found her."

"It was a tense situation," Cara said, not looking up from the stack of case files in her arms, shuffling through them as if they were more important than the case at hand. "I'm sure it was a one-time thing."

Matt removed the single folder he had tucked under his arm and set it on the end of the conference table where they stood. Opening it, he began spreading photos out as he spoke. "There were stacks of books, journals, and blankets in that closet. Bev stayed in that closet because the rest of the house was a pigsty."

"Not to mention," Jamie mentioned, "Deidra's brother was using Bev, a fourteen-year-old minor, to blackmail another minor into committing felonies on his behalf."

"That's not been proven," Cara said, looking anywhere but at them or the photos on the table.

"Are you Deidra's lawyer now?"

"Of course not. I'm just trying to find a place for Beverly to land."

Matt pointed at the photos, then didn't speak again until Cara looked. She couldn't hide her cringe. "That place?" Matt said.

"With two addicts," Jamie pressed, "who are both in custody and experiencing significant withdrawal symptoms consistent with long-term daily drug use."

"Good." Cara lifted her wide blue eyes from the photos —and continued grasping at straws. "First step to turning their lives around."

"Like your brother?" Aidan's voice was as sharp as a whip. He strode into the room, Rooster on his heels. "The federal prosecutor here"—he said with a tilt of his head toward Rooster—"made some calls. Your brother, an associate of Darien White, is at MCJ serving time for manufacturing and trafficking meth. Blew up a house and everything. Your mother's, in fact, less than a month after she died, which means he was manufacturing it well before her death. Wonder if that had anything to do with her declining health?"

Cara blanched as pale as her white-blond hair.

"Did you think we wouldn't find out?" Aidan said.

"The two . . . the two weren't connected," she stuttered.

"We'll see about that," Rooster said. "In any event, you're done here. Ms. Kildare's case has been reassigned. You should also check in with your supervisor. Pretty sure you're done with social services too."

Her face crumpled. "I was just trying to do my job." Jamie was ninety-nine-point-nine percent certain her tears were for herself and not for Bev's welfare or the welfare of the children in the files she clutched to her chest.

"Negligently, at best," Rooster said. "Intentional misconduct and bribery at worst, and my office will find out. Now leave those files and get out."

She slung the files on the table, contents scattering, as little care for those kids' cases as she'd shown for Bev's, then turned on her heel and bolted. "You want eyes on her?" Matt asked. "Ten to one she runs."

"I would not take that bet," Aidan said, stepping next to Jamie and nestling a hand in the small of his back, reconnecting and bringing Jamie's ire down with a simple touch. That was usually Jamie's job, but in this partnership, he needed Aidan to steady him sometimes too.

"I'm not taking that bet either," Rooster agreed. "Eyes on, please," he said to Matt. "Maybe she leads us somewhere else."

Matt slipped out of the room, and Jamie began to reassemble the discarded files, Aidan and Rooster helping. "This case does seem to twist and turn back onto itself," Jamie remarked. "How're the kids?"

"Good," Aidan answered. "They're in the break room

doing homework. Tricia's on her way over," he said to Rooster. "Once she gets here, you can ask them what you need. They'll cooperate. They only cut school today because Cara called Bev and told her she was going to place her back with Deidra. Bev knew where to find the dirt to prevent that."

"More than the list on the wall you texted me?"

"Attic full of stolen goods," Aidan said, first showing Jamie a picture on his phone—boxes and boxes of stolen goods—before showing the same to Rooster. "Berat is still at the house with the CSU unit Rick brought over. They'll print everything, then load it up for evidence."

"So not just a one-time thing for White?" Jamie said.

"Definitely not. Anything on Arty or the hack?"

"Arty's dead."

They all spun toward the new voice, one Jamie couldn't remember hearing in well over a year. In that time, Sutton Conder had apparently traded his fitted suit and briefcase for jeans, a tee, and a backpack, his regulation haircut for overlong strands streaked with silver and blond, and a honeyed tan that spoke of time spent someplace sunny versus countless hours under office fluorescents. Yet despite all those outward signs of a less stressful life than his old one as SAC of the Bureau's organized crime unit, Sutton looked downright antsy. Hands shoved in his pockets, eyes darting around the room, it was almost like he wasn't sure how to be in the office or around people anymore.

Aidan barreled right through whatever was making the former SAC so uncomfortable. "Well, look who the cat dragged in," he said, approaching with a smile and outstretched hand. "Where have you been hiding, Agent

Conder? I thought for sure we'd have seen you at Marsh and Levi's wedding."

Jamie and Aidan had both worked cases with Sutton before, most recently the summer before last when Aidan had helped Sutton and Charlie nail the human traffickers Levi and Marsh had been after. In doing so, they'd also exposed a corrupt congressman who'd been a presidential hopeful. Unfortunately, Sutton had lost his job in the process.

"You can drop the agent now," he said as he shook Aidan's hand, some of the wariness fading. "As for the wedding, I was afraid if I showed, your former boss would recruit me. She's relentless."

"Mel knows talent when she sees it, and you're one of the best when it comes to organized crime."

"Charlie's catching up fast," he said with an approving smile for his protégé. "But she's tied up on a major bust, so she sent me, unofficially, with a care package."

"Wait?" Rooster said. "Are you *the* Sutton Conder who ran organized crimes for the Bureau and took down Stewart Anthony?"

"The same," Sutton said, offering his hand. "Took down myself too, but I still count it a win."

"Henry Roos, AUSA," the prosecutor introduced himself. "And you should count it a win. You did this state a favor getting rid of Anthony. That man was awful, as a politician and a human."

"No argument here," Sutton said, relaxing further, sensing Rooster, the unknown variable in the room, was a supporter and not a detractor. He exchanged hellos and handshakes with Jamie too, then slung his backpack into one of the chairs. "Though I'm afraid none of you will be happy to see me once I tell you what I know."

"You mean there's more than 'Arty's dead'?" Aidan said.

Jamie raked a hand through his hair. "Does this have anything to do with me tracing the Talley hack back to his brother, Michael Martino?"

"You did?" Aidan said, whipping his gaze back to Jamie.

"Sorry, Bev was the bigger concern when you first got here."

"As she should have been," Aidan agreed. "But now that that's at least temporarily resolved, sounds like we've got bigger problems."

"You do." Sutton withdrew several folders from his bag. "That care package I mentioned." He dropped the first folder on the table. "Everyone's been getting in on the cargo theft game, and the Mafia have been doing it in one form or another for a very long time."

"High-end jobs?" Matt said, reentering the room and giving Sutton a pat on the back. "Good to see you, man." They'd worked more closely on the trafficking case with Marsh and Levi, Matt partnered with Levi then, and if Jamie had to guess, they'd been in touch since. Would maybe even guess Sutton was local now, given his tan and quick appearance on scene.

"*All* jobs," Sutton said.

"But why would they outsource *any* of their jobs to someone like White?" Aidan said. "Especially high-end ones like those diamonds."

"He got in debt to them," Matt said. "He told us that. So

Pudge let him run some cargo thefts. If he gets pinched, he's deadweight."

"But then White starts skimming," Jamie reasoned. "And Pudge finds out."

"So, time to make him dead," Rooster concluded. "At that handoff for the diamonds. With not-Arty-Martino."

Aidan leaned into Jamie's side. "That could have been Angel."

Arm around his waist, Jamie steadied his husband, while across from them, Rooster fumed. "I am definitely putting manslaughter on White's charge sheet. Maybe more."

"Do you know who Pudge is?" Jamie asked Sutton. "Who the meet might have actually been with?"

"Don't know on the second. As for Pudge . . ." Sutton dropped another file on the table. "Patrick Mason. Not Italian but a known associate of the LA Mafia. His family is loaded. He's well connected. Never gets pinched. Gets others like White to do his dirty work."

Aidan pulled the folder closer, Jamie reading over his shoulder at the thefts Patrick Mason was suspected of being involved with. Dozens between Los Angeles and Vegas. "Did we"—Aidan glanced up—"Talley Enterprises, I mean, just get caught up in their theft spree?"

Sutton added another folder, the thinnest of the three, to the stack. "No, you have a vulnerability. Tomás Diaz."

Jamie recognized the name immediately. "I spoke with Tomás an hour ago. He runs tech support for TE's Long Beach and LA operations. If he had a record, it would have popped in the background checks." TE's vetting process was extensive. They'd put Jamie through the wringer when he'd been brought on to help design various tech and security programs and protocols for their flagship vessel, the *Ellen*.

"Diaz has no record," Sutton said. "Nor is he a known associate of the Martinos or the Mafia. But some quick work by Agent Hall to refine the search you'd already started turned up a connection. Diaz and Michael Martino were in night school together. Computer science."

"Shit," Jamie cursed, and Aidan angled his direction.

"If you spoke to him an hour ago," Aidan said, "I assume it was about the hack?"

Jamie nodded. "I asked for all the activity logs from the week prior to the second theft."

"How would you approach this?" Matt asked Sutton. "This could be a big bust. We don't want to spook Martino or the Mafia before we have all our ducks in a row."

"I wouldn't go after Martino. Not Pudge yet either," Sutton replied, then said to Aidan, "You going after your own internal leak, though, that makes sense. Get Diaz to talk. Clean record like that"—he jutted his chin at Diaz's folder—"I'd bet he doesn't want to be a part of this."

"Where was he an hour ago?" Aidan asked Jamie.

"TE office at Long Beach with KJ," Jamie said as he gathered up Sutton's prelim files. "Thanks for these," he said to the former agent. "And tell Lauren thanks too."

"We'll ring Rick from the car," Aidan said. "Have him meet us there." He was halfway to the door when he halted, Jamie practically crashing into him. "Fuck, the kids."

"I've got them," Matt and Rooster said at the same time.

"No, we can—" Jamie started.

"Go." Matt waved them on. "Tricia is here, and so is Ward, plus me, and Rooster. Berat will be back soon too.

And we've got Sutton to give them dry land surfing lessons if all else fails to entertain them."

Aidan's gaze swung to the former agent so fast that Jamie laughed out loud. "Did you miss the tan, babe?"

Sutton laughed too. "Go," he echoed Matt. "I'll coordinate on the Mafia angle. I may even give Mel a call for some of that off-the-books info she's so good at getting."

"She'll have her claws in you then for sure," Aidan said.

"Was only a matter of time."

TWENTY-ONE

Jamie entered the office conference room ahead of Rick and Aidan. Among the three of them, he was the only familiar face to Tomás. They'd spoken on the phone not long ago and had met in person earlier in the day. The midthirties IT tech had been friendly each of those times. His smile now was friendly too, but his dark eyes, shifting between Rick and Aidan, gave away how nervous he truly was. As did the initial shake in his voice and hand as he held the latter out to Jamie. "Didn't expect to see you back so soon."

"We had some follow-up questions," Jamie said, then introduced Rick and Aidan, the tech's eyes growing wide at Aidan's last name.

"I'm here as an agent first," Aidan said. "A Talley second."

That didn't seem to make Tomás feel any better as he sank into the chair beside KJ. Before he could spiral into worst-case scenarios that would likely be proven correct by the time this conversation was over, Jamie drew Tomás's attention back to him and the world Tomás knew best, even if it had been the one that had likely gotten him into trouble. "I wanted to chat more tech specs, specifically about the process of confirming off-loading instructions."

"The bills of lading."

"Right," Jamie said. "KJ told us any paper bills are checked against the digital ones in TE's system."

"That's correct."

"And how are those digital ones submitted?"

"Through TE's online portal, Steele. You know, the one you designed," he said to Jamie with a chuckle that Jamie returned, keeping up the pretense of computer geeks in league together. Whatever it took to keep Tomás talking. "Customers can track their goods in transit, through customs, and make whatever pick-up or delivery arrangements they need. All our port operations and ships now have some version of the program you designed for the *Ellen*."

"Each user still has to go through multi-factor authentication?"

Tomás nodded. "Unique IDs, strong passwords, two-factor, the whole bit."

"And what about when someone needs to change something in the original bill of lading? Like for a new carrier on the delivery, a new destination. Is there a shortcut?"

Tomás straightened in his chair, his answer coming not so quickly, more deliberately. "No shortcut," he said. "The user has to go through the same process." He paused to wet his lips, maybe also to mentally run through his story. To check the lies against the truth. "Once an update is submitted, it's flagged in the system and someone on our end checks and clears it."

"And what's your role in this?" Aidan asked.

"Well, sir," he said, eyes shifting back and forth between Aidan and Jamie, "I run tech support for the port here and the one across the way in LA. So if one of our employees or users runs into an issue with our tech systems or equipment, they email or text the help desk, a ticket is created, and it's routed to my team. Nine times out of ten the solution is to restart the program or device," he said with a chuckle, albeit a weaker one than he'd given Jamie earlier.

"So you wouldn't normally handle help desk matters?" Rick said.

Tomás's gaze whipped to him, then, as if realizing how guilty the movement had appeared, shifted his body the same direction, crossing his legs. "Sometimes I have to if we're slammed. Or if something important like this comes up."

"Let's go back to the change orders," Jamie said. "Does your team review those?"

"No, that's the transport agents."

"And what's that process look like?"

"KJ would have to answer that," he said, sitting straighter and lifting his chin, thinking he'd found an out. "As I said, we're not involved."

KJ didn't flinch when all eyes turned on her; she had no reason to. "The transfer agent double-checks the IP address, the authentication, and that all protocols were followed," she explained. "And if the total value of the shipment being transported is over a certain dollar threshold, they call the client to confirm the change."

"Was the dollar value of the shipment stolen yesterday over the threshold?" Aidan asked.

"Yes, it was."

"Was the client called in this case?"

"According to the paperwork, yes."

"Except the client never got a call," Rick said as he pulled a file from his tattered bag and set it on the table. He opened it and slid a single sheet across the table. "Their call records from the date of the change order. No calls from TE extensions."

"And this case was routed to *your* help desk," Jamie said to Tomás. Rick produced another sheet of paper; a ticket from the TE system. "One of those rare times?"

"Sometimes we assist if the system gets hung up."

Aidan leaned forward in his chair, forearms on the table. "What do you mean by 'hung up'?"

Beads of sweat dotted Tomás's hairline. "Sometimes the gateway times out."

"And you personally stepped in on this one," Jamie said. "That's what the activity logs show."

"It was a Tuesday," he said. "We're typically slammed on Tuesdays."

"Good day to cover something up," Aidan remarked.

He shook his head a little too enthusiastically. "I have no idea what you're talking about."

"Rick, do you have that activity log?" Jamie said, and Rick passed him several pieces of paper. He flipped them around so Tomás was forced to look at the highlighted entries. "Just before the altered papers came in on Monday, someone on the user's end changed the two-factor contact info for the user who submitted the change. And when the new paperwork was submitted, the gateway timed out. It got routed to you, and you approved it. All within a thirty-minute window."

"That sounds like a hack on the user's end."

"By Michael Martino," Aidan said, and the color bled from Tomás's face. "Did you think we'd just assume he did it all by himself?" Aidan shook his head. "He needed help on this end too."

"I built the system for accountability," Jamie added.

"I don't—" Tomás started, then stopped. Swallowed hard. "I don't know who that is." The shake in his voice betrayed him again.

"Except you do, Tomás. Michael Martino was your classmate in night school."

"And about a month ago," Rick said, producing another sheet of paper, "your sister who owns a bakery filed a complaint with LBPD about being harassed for protection money. She didn't know who it was, but the description she gave matches Martino. But then the complaint was withdrawn before LBPD could investigate."

Tomás ran a hand through his hair. Lowered it. And when it wouldn't stop shaking, he clasped it with the other in front of him.

KJ laid a hand over his. "You've been a model employee," she said, voice steady and gentle. "Don't let this ruin it."

"I can keep my job?"

"I can't make that promise," she said. "Only Danny and Siobhan can."

"But if you tell us what you know about Martino," Aidan said, "I can at least tell you, as an FBI agent and as a Talley, that we won't press charges."

Propping both elbows on the table, he covered his face with his hands, his shoulders heavy as he gutted out broken words. "I just wanted to protect her. That bakery is her dream."

"Then tell us what we need to know, Tomás," Jamie said, mirroring KJ's tone. "Let's make sure that dream doesn't die."

TWENTY-TWO

Bev leaned around Aidan's side, staring into the potato pot he was dumping more cabbage into. "What exactly is that?"

"Colcannon," he replied, his accent thicker. It was impossible not to unfurl the brogue on the name of the dish he'd heard spoken, had watched made more times than he could count, the Irish staple his father's favorite.

Bev's not so much, judging by the way she wrinkled her nose. "Why can't we just have potatoes?"

Aidan gave her the same excuse his parents had given him and his siblings whenever they'd protested. "The cabbage makes them healthier for you."

"Marginally," Jamie called from the balcony where he had a chicken on the grill.

"You almost done, traitor?" Aidan called back, as he continued to mash potatoes and cabbage into the simmering cream, garlic, and leeks.

"Five minutes or so, dear."

Smiling, Aidan glanced up in time to see Angel step beside Jamie, tablet in hand. "Can we make this mod?"

"Good idea," Jamie said with a nod. "Make it lighter and faster."

"That was my thought."

"Yeah, I think we can do that."

"Cool." Angel went back to tapping the tablet screen as he sank onto the outdoor sofa beside his mother.

Aidan, however, was stuck back on Angel's "we." He couldn't help but smile wider at the implication, whether it was intentional or not.

"I see you," Bev sing-songed as she moved around the kitchen, pulling plates out of the cabinets and silverware from the drawers.

He let his smile grow wider; no use hiding it. "I missed him."

"He missed you too. He also misses having family around."

"So he made one at school?" Aidan asked, recalling his and Jamie's conversation with Izzy yesterday.

"Yeah, he did, but when he started hanging out with me, some of his friends ghosted him. Thought we were together, and so he wasn't 'really gay.'" Aidan expected her to roll her eyes at the ignorance of their friends, but instead, she rested back against the island, chin lowered. "I feel bad about it."

"Angel made his choice." Aidan set aside the potato masher and dipped his own chin low enough to catch her gaze. "And so far, it seems like a good one to me."

She glanced up at him through her lashes, and there was the spark of rebel he expected. "Except that whole theft and speeding thing." She cut her glare outside to where Angel was at Jamie's side, excitedly asking about another engine mod. "That's not gonna help the speeding," she said.

Aidan laughed. "Probably not." He slid a spoon from Bev's grip and dipped it into the potato pot. "Try it," he said, offering her the spoon in exchange for the plates. Aidan wished he'd recorded the reactions that played across her face. From maybe-not-so-bad to eww-why to I-found-another-bit-of-buttery-goodness.

"It's not as bad as I expected," she admitted. "But the slimy cabbage is gonna take some getting used to."

Aidan liked the sound of that as much as he liked Angel's "we." Both kids were assuming Aidan and Jamie would remain in their lives after this case was over, which was more than Aidan dared hope for, more than he would've thought possible if you'd asked him Saturday how things would go. Letting his smile loose again, he pitched the spoon in the sink and grabbed a serving bowl for the potatoes while Bev set the table. Expertly. Not something Aidan could imagine her doing at Deidra's. A foster before, or her parents, maybe? Or was this another Internet thing? In any event, not his place to ask something that personal. Yet. He kept things more general, for now. "How are you doing with everything?" he asked. "Feeling less damsel-like?"

"Gucci, for now." She came back to the kitchen for the spoon she was short. "I'm sure it'll all hit in a few days, but right now, it's kind of surreal. To get out of that place and land at a boujee one like this." She waved the utensil in the air, gesturing around them. "And you and Jamie seem like decent folk, even if you both work too much."

"Not gonna deny that," he said, acknowledging her correct perception about them. "And Bev . . ." He waited for her to glance up before he acknowledged the likely correct prediction she'd also made about herself. "When it does hit, talk to one of us, or to Izzy, or to your new social worker."

"I trust y'all more than I do him," she said as she rose on her tiptoes to grab glasses out of the cabinet over the microwave.

She managed to get down four, and Aidan grabbed the fifth. "Jamie's running background checks. Rooster too."

"He *so* looks like a Rooster. Not as mean as I thought one would be, but the hair and the suit and the strut." She mimicked the prosecutor's walk as she carried the glasses to the table, and Aidan laughed out loud, drawing Jamie's attention.

Y'all good? he mouthed. His blue eyes sparkled under the balcony string lights, and his smile was wide and easy. Despite the chaos still circling around them, he was helping to center them all, insisting on a "family" dinner at the home they were borrowing tonight.

Better than, he mouthed back with a wink.

Bev groaned. "How long have y'all been married?"

"Five years, very happily. And that's twice you've used y'all," he said to Bev as he carried the potatoes over to the table. "But there's no accent when you say it."

"I like it. It's more gender neutral."

"Agree, but most folks have to train themselves to use it." Aidan would often notice a pause, no matter how short, as a person mentally made the switch before saying it. Granted, kids adapted to changes in language and customs more quickly than adults, but Aidan didn't think that was all here. "It comes more naturally to you, like it does Jamie, who grew up in North Carolina."

Bev lowered herself into one of the dining room chairs, quiet, and Aidan immediately regretted the topic, realizing maybe this was a step too far. "Bev, you don't have to—"

"My mom was from Georgia," she said as she tumbled the small butter knife through her fingers, her voice muted. "Dad was from California. I grew up out here, but certain words of hers stuck."

That was more of her past than she owed any of them at this point, and Aidan didn't want to linger there either, especially when it so clearly darkened her mood. Catching a whiff of the potatoes, he knew the perfect segue to cheer her up. "My brother Danny is like that," he said. "I was twelve when we moved from Ireland to California, but he was just a toddler. He grew up here, but being around us and our parents, he uses certain words and pronounces them no way a native Californian would."

Curiosity brightened her big brown eyes. "Like what?"

Grinning, he withdrew his phone and dialed his brother.

"Hey, big bro," Danny answered, practically shouting over shipyard noises in the background. "I'll be there Thursday morning."

"Good," Aidan said. "But I wasn't calling about that. Need you to do me a quick favor."

"What?"

"What's Dad's favorite dish?"

"Colcannon," he answered immediately, a touch of the brogue in his voice that was rarely ever there.

Bev laughed, eyes wide. "No fucking way. Say it again."

"Colcannon."

"That's wild."

Across the table, Aidan laughed, and when Danny spoke, he could hear the smile in his brother's voice too. "You're making fun of me, aren't you?"

"Just a demonstration on accents," Aidan said. "Love you, baby bro."

"Love you too. See you tomorrow. Gotta run." The tail end of his sign-off was muffled by a blasting foghorn, which he thankfully silenced by ending the call.

"Your family's tight?" She could have simply made the observation, as most folks did. The Talleys didn't hide their affections for one another; they'd learned not to when the Troubles had stolen their oldest sibling. But Bev had phrased her observation as a question, one Aidan sensed was part curiosity, part caution.

"Yes, we're close," he said. "But not to the exclusion of new family members." He held her gaze that came alive with hope. "We have a way of collecting strays. Ask Danny's wife or Jamie's or my best friends sometime."

Her small nod felt like one of Aidan's greatest victories.

Another of those victories walked through the balcony door with a piping hot bird teetering on a beer can surrounded by vegetables in the cast iron skillet he carried between mitts.

Angel was on his heels, heaving a beleaguered "Finally," which earned him a shoulder swat from his mother.

"You act like I don't feed you," she said.

Aidan knew that not to be true now, even if the thought had crossed his mind early on, given Angel's baggy clothes and lanky frame. The latter was just biology—the boy had eaten regularly each day, not like he was starving, not like he was forcing himself—and the former just seemed to be his preference.

Angel plopped into the chair beside Bev, Izzy the chair on the other side of her. Her light brown eyes glanced up at Aidan, and before the words were out, Aidan knew what she was going to say. Her "You couldn't just make regular potatoes?" was muffled by laughter as he tossed a dishtowel across the table at her.

"That's what I said!" Bev concurred, and that earned her a balled-up napkin, everyone laughing louder.

Jamie appeared beside Aidan, veggies in a bowl he set on the table. "I'll eat your cabbage potatoes, baby." He kissed his cheek, then rotated back to the island to finish breaking down the chicken. "Any word from Matt or Rick?" he asked when Aidan joined him.

Aidan shook his head. "Maybe the traffic to County was bad." At his arraignment today, White had been remanded to County lockup. Matt and Rick were headed there this evening to question him about Pudge, the Martinos, and whomever else he was working with.

Jamie finished with the chicken and brought the platter of crispy-skinned goodness to the table. They'd all just finished cleaning their plates, Aidan chewing through his last juicy bite, when a knock sounded at the door.

Jamie started to rise, but Aidan beat him to it, resting a hand on his shoulder. "Stay, I've got it. Ask Izzy about the first time she tried colcannon."

Translation: Keep them distracted.

Jamie read him loud and clear, his "I gotta hear this" instantly engaging.

Aidan didn't have time to retrieve his weapon from the home office safe, nor would he want to with the kids in the room, so as discreetly as possible, he palmed the knife Jamie had used to slice the chicken, holding it up against his forearm as he made his way to the door and checked the peephole.

Matt stood directly outside the door, Rick and Berat in

the background behind him. He laid the knife on the foyer table, then slipped outside, concern ratcheting up at seeing Ward there too. "I thought we gave you the night off."

"He's back on the kids and Izzy," Matt said. "Twenty-four seven."

"Why's that?" Aidan asked, certain whatever news they were here to deliver couldn't be good.

"Darien and Deidra White are dead."

TWENTY-THREE

"Is everything okay?" Izzy asked as Jamie started the coffee brewing.

Aidan had summoned him to the foyer, filled him in, then, leaving Ward at the door, had led the rest of the group out to the balcony, shutting the door behind them. Jamie had volunteered to get the coffee and make sure Izzy and the kids were settled. The latter he distracted with his tablet and a mission to order holiday decorations for the condo, a surprise they would leave behind for Press when he returned. Izzy, however, was not so easily put off the scent. Regardless of Tom's and Aidan's efforts, she had been an LEO's partner, and she had the Spidey senses that went with it.

"Development on the case," Jamie told her. "It was quicker for them to come here than for me and Aidan to go back to the office."

She shot him a look that screamed *Bullshit* without making a sound. Part of the reason they'd pinged Press about using his place was its proximity to the office; Izzy had to realize that too. She stopped short of calling him on the lie, though, and moved on to making the necessary plans. "I'm off tomorrow," she said. "But I'm supposed to be on a red-eye Thursday night to JFK. Down to Miami the next day, then back here on Saturday."

"I'd cancel it."

"I hated this part of the job." She grabbed another mug from the cabinet, filled it three quarters full of milk, then added it to the ones Jamie was pouring coffee into. "Well, at least we can go to Maryanne's party now."

Jamie shot her a *What now?* version of the look she'd shot him earlier.

"She's a close friend," she answered. "I'll get you and Aidan the info to clear it, and Ward can come too. I'm sure no one will mind the eye candy."

Jamie chuckled as he loaded mugs onto a tray. "Maybe this will all be over tomorrow. You can go to the party and take a worry-free weekend with the kids."

"That would be glorious," Izzy said, claiming her own mug, then laying her other hand on his on the tray handle. She waited for him to glance up, and when he did, Jamie found her brown eyes swirling with worry and guilt. "I think the world of Bev," she said quietly. "She's the sibling Angel's always wanted, but I don't think the courts would give me custody. I'm single, work a job that puts me frequently out of the home, and while we're financially afloat, it's more like swimming upstream."

Jamie released the tray so he could take Izzy's free hand in both of his, giving it a squeeze. "Let's just worry about this week for now. We'll sort out the rest when the time comes." That was all any of them could do, even if his mind was running away with scenes of future family Christmases.

Nodding, she inhaled deep, lifted her chin, and walked with him to the balcony door, opening it so he could carry out the tray of drinks.

"Izzy okay?" Aidan asked once she'd closed the door behind him.

"She was married to an agent. She knows something's up." He set the coffees down on the table, and everyone descended like sharks on chum. "She's off tomorrow but was supposed to be in the air Thursday through Saturday. I suggested she cancel it."

"Probably for the best," Matt said.

Jamie snagged the last mug, then claimed the cushion next to Aidan. "So, what do we know?"

"By the time we got to County," Rick said, "a fight had broken out, and Darien was killed in the melee."

"And Deidra?"

"Withdrawal-related complications."

"Do we believe that?" Aidan said.

Berat shook his head. "Not in the least."

"Was anyone else killed?" Jamie asked.

"One other inmate," Rick said. "The person who shivved White. He ran at the guard coming to break it up."

"Suicide by cop."

"Likely."

"Mob associate?" Aidan asked.

Berat nodded.

"They're cleaning up loose ends."

"Those kids are loose ends," Rick said with a nod toward Angel and Bev at the dining table, their heads together over Jamie's tablet. At Aidan's answering growl,

Rick held his hands up, palms out, fingers spread. "No offense, boss. Just the truth."

The jazz hands, intentional or not, had the welcome effect of diffusing some of the tension, the corner of Aidan's mouth twitching as he fought a smile. Jamie laid a hand on his husband's knee and moved the conversation on. "Who else is left?"

"Tomás and his sister," Matt replied. "Already put them in protective custody."

"Which leaves Pudge and Michael Martino," Aidan said.

"I think we move on Pudge," Rick said. "I've been going through Agent Con—Sutton's—files." He passed the one he'd carried in under his arm across the table to Aidan. "Martino has a beef with the Bureau after what happened to his brother. He's less likely to talk than Pudge."

"Do we have a location on Mason?"

Rick jutted his chin at the folder spread across Aidan's lap. "List of his known haunts are in there," he said. "So are his credit card numbers and banking information."

Jamie snatched the file out of Aidan's hands and stood. "If he's used anything but cash at any of these locations, I'll know in thirty."

"Prep teams to cover," Aidan said as the rest of them rose. "Let's be ready to move as soon as we have a location."

TWENTY-FOUR

Turned out Pudge was at none of his usual haunts. "Well," Aidan said as he peered through a pair of binoculars, "this is far more civilized than I imagined for a wannabe mobster called Pudge." Across Grand Avenue, Patrick Mason was among the finely dressed one-percenters eating canapés and sipping champagne in Broad Plaza. The mini park next to LA's contemporary art museum had been decked out for the holiday charity gala, with fairy lights in the trees, fake snow on the ground, and giant ornaments at the corner nearest the museum's entrance.

"It's a lot of people," Jamie said from the driver's seat where he was looking through his own set of lenses. "*His* people. He's protecting himself."

His people was right, Pudge's parents the sponsors of tonight's gala. When there'd been no hits on Pudge's credit or bank accounts, they'd scoured his and his parents' social media feeds, seeing the event tonight mentioned on both. Sure enough, Aidan watched as the freckled man with chestnut hair and blue eyes chatted animatedly with the blond stunner on his arm and another couple. Pudge was thin, like White had described him, like the pictures Sutton had showed them, but seeing him next to others, the strength in his wiry limbs was more obvious, his posture impeccable. Upbringing and muscle tone and no evident discomfort at having been shoved into a tux for the evening. "How the hell did this guy get tangled up with the mob?" Aidan wondered aloud.

"Rich kid looking for a thrill," Matt speculated from the phone in the dash holder. He and Rick were parked at the other end of the plaza, at the bottom of the stairs that led to the surface and access streets that ran along and below the plaza.

"Probably how it started," Jamie said. "As for how it's going, that's the boss's daughter on his arm."

Aidan nearly dropped the binoculars. "That's who she is?" He hadn't had nearly enough time with Sutton's file to do a deep dive. "Little boss or big boss?"

Jamie flipped through said file and produced several surveillance photos of the couple. "Big boss. That's Lara Russo, Orlando Russo's only child."

"Is Russo here?"

"Near the ornaments," Berat radioed from where he was stationed on the plaza, dressed as one of the party's hired security guards. "Late fifties, five-ten, salt and pepper hair. Fit too, like he spends too much time in his home gym."

Aidan raised the binoculars again and located Russo, a brick of an older gentleman in a tailored tux, chatting with several other patrons, one a celebrity in an all-black tux that Aidan vaguely recognized but couldn't quite place. It took another few seconds to find the happy couple again a dozen or so feet away, mid-crowd with a different couple. Judging by their resemblance to Pudge, Aidan guessed they were Patrick's parents. "Bet Russo likes being seen with the city's big-money players."

"Makes him seem legitimate too," Matt said, echoing the direction of Aidan's thoughts.

Aidan continued to watch the scene unfold. Black ties, glittery dresses, crystal, and caviar. LA's elite and the mob wanted a piece of it too. All of that made sense. One thing, however, did not. "Why would *any* of these people deal with someone like Darien White?"

"It's like with the kids," Jamie said. "What's missing?"

"We'll have to figure it out later," Berat said. "Something's up."

Aidan whipped his binoculars back up. Pudge had stepped away from his parents and Lara and stood on the edge of the crowd, facing away from them with his phone to his ear. Shoulders hunched, Pudge plowed a hand into his hair, ruining the gelled do.

"Something didn't go as planned," Jamie said.

And continued to go south as Orlando hustled Pudge's direction, the boss flanked by two guys even bigger than him. Orlando grabbed Pudge by the biceps and hauled him farther away from the crowd, out of hearing range. Whatever he said, it was short, not sweet, and made Pudge turn ghostly pale. Orlando snapped one more thing in Pudge's face, spittle flying, then practically threw the younger man at his guards. He disappeared back into the crowd, leaving his muscle to drag Pudge the opposite direction, toward the back plaza stairs. "Matt, Rick, you're up."

"I'm trailing," Berat said.

"We're pulling around," Jamie said as he cranked the car

and pulled into traffic, crossing lanes to turn left onto 2nd Street. "Think that was about White?"

"If it was," Aidan said, "then I'm more confused than ever, because that looked like Pudge getting chewed out for *not* following orders." Jamie was right; they were missing some piece of the puzzle.

"They're taking him down the stairs," Berat reported. "On foot."

"Matt, Rick," Aidan said. "Move in on foot." He reached through the seats for his vest, then hauled it on and tightened the straps. "We have to get the jump on the muscle if we're going to take Patrick without word getting back to the boss it was us."

"Roger that."

"We're swinging around onto Hope Street," Jamie said.

"Going silent," Matt reported, followed by Berat's, "They're turning onto GTK Way."

"That's the access street below the plaza," Jamie said as he pulled the car to the curb just shy of the street's entrance.

Aidan reached across the console, palming his knee. "Whiskey, I need—"

"Me to stay in the car, I know." Jamie hauled him in by the vest strap for a quick, hard kiss. "Be careful. I'll block the entrance here."

He exited the car and darted into the lower-level access street, hanging close to the left side wall, in the shadows so as not to attract attention. At this hour, though GTK was mostly empty, just staff cars and delivery trucks waiting to load up after the party in the plaza was over.

Up ahead, Matt and Rick were on the far side of an alcove opening, Berat the side Aidan was approaching from. Matt signaled for Aidan to fall in behind Berat, who was holding a wine bottle he must have snagged from upstairs. This close, Aidan could hear the struggle inside the dark alcove—grunts, curses, fists connecting with skin and bone.

They didn't have time to waste.

Across from him, Matt nodded his agreement and drew his weapon. Once he and Rick were in similar ready positions, Aidan whispered, "Now," to Berat.

The detective tossed the bottle into the street, the glass shattering.

One more crack of bone, one final grunt, then the commotion inside the alcove ceased.

The person who emerged was not the one Aidan had expected. Bloody and bruised, bow tie gone, flecks of red dotting his torn white shirt, Patrick "Pudge" Mason hobbled out of the shadows, one arm dangling from a shoulder that was clearly out of its socket, his other fist raised, ready to go again if he had to.

"Patrick Mason?" Aidan called.

Pudge wiped his split lip with the back of his fist. "Who's asking?"

"Special Agent Aidan Talley."

"Oh shit." He spun on his heel, then wobbled to a stop when a groan sounded from farther back in the alcove.

"There's nowhere to run, man," Matt said. "Do you want to be on your own or with us when they come to?"

"Patrick," Aidan said. "We can help you."

"Fuck," Pudge cursed, then with a groan of his own dragged himself the rest of the way out of the alcove. "You can't take me to the station. I'll be dead for sure, then."

"You don't think you are already?"

He coughed, then winced and grabbed at his shoulder. "I don't even know what the fuck is going on."

"We can sort it somewhere else," Berat said. "We need to move before Russo realizes everyone's missing."

Matt tipped his head toward the street's exit. "I know someplace nearby."

TWENTY-FIVE

Jamie checked once more that the rental was locked, then left it parked behind Matt and Rick's cruiser at the mouth of the alley they'd turned into a few streets over from GTK. Like that access street, the alley they were in was lower-level too, and as Jamie followed their group further into it, the already narrow street narrowed further. Only wide enough for foot traffic and barely wide enough for Jamie's shoulders at that. They descended a short, metal flight of stairs, and twenty or so feet ahead, old-fashioned, flame-lit porch lamps flickered on either side of a door, a wooden sign that read Remedy hanging overhead. But instead of continuing to that door, they entered through a closer one in the recessed stone wall, Matt punching in a code on the door's digital keypad to gain access.

As Jamie pushed closed the heavy metal door, Aidan glanced back over his shoulder, curiosity swirling in his brown eyes. Matty Kim had some beans to spill, but that interrogation would have to wait for a time when they weren't in the company of a rogue wannabe mobster.

"Hey, you can't be—"

Willowy was the first word that came to Jamie's mind about the man who'd appeared at the end of the hallway ahead of them. Tall, leanly muscled, with long hair that flowed in rock star waves over his shoulders. As Matt stepped closer to the stranger, *brother* was the second word that came to Jamie's mind. At first glance, they couldn't look more different—Matt in a suit and tie, his black hair neat, his sidearm his only accessory; the stranger in torn jeans and a tank, his hair black at the roots then dyed blond to the ends, his fingers loaded with chunky rings and his wrists adorned with dozens of bracelets—but the arch of their noses, their thinner upper lips over fuller bottom ones, the stubborn jut of their chins were exactly the same.

"Can we use the back room?" Matt asked. "I wouldn't ask if it wasn't an emergency." He shifted enough for his brother to see the beat-up and bruised man in the middle of their group.

His brother grimaced. "First aid kit's in the bathroom. Clean up on your way out, otherwise Ryan'll shit." He didn't wait for a reply. Just turned and vanished around the corner, a door closing and locking in his wake.

A deep breath later, Matt opened the door to their right and led them into a surprisingly large hangout space with a piano in one corner, a table and chairs in the other, various other instruments on stands, and a large U-shaped sectional that took up most of the room. Matt disappeared into the attached bathroom while Rick propped Pudge against the edge of the table.

Jamie stepped in front of him. "You want me to fix that arm?" As a former player and FBI agent, it wouldn't be his first time popping one back into joint; as a coach, he'd watched the trainers do it more than a few times.

"Fucking hell," Pudge gritted out, then nodded anyway.

Jamie didn't give him a chance to second-guess his decision. Grabbing the wrist of his injured arm, Jamie lifted it and yanked it forward while Rick held Pudge in place by the other shoulder.

"Fucking hell!" he shouted decibels louder, and Matt came running out of the bathroom.

"Keep him quiet!"

"It's over," Jamie said as he helped Pudge out of his jacket now that he'd regained some mobility. "That should be the worst of it." He fashioned a sling out of the jacket, then worked with Matt and Rick to clean up their suspect.

"You really have no idea what's going on?" Aidan asked.

Pudge's blue eyes bounced around the gathered group before landing back on Aidan. "I don't know what I can say here without incriminating myself."

"Five minutes free," Matt said. He stepped over to the piano, lifted the lid, and removed a timer. The way he said it, the way he knew exactly where that timer was, gave Jamie the distinct impression it wasn't Matt's first time at his ruse. Or in this room. He cranked the timer, then set the device on the table beside Pudge. "Clock's ticking."

"Who did you get a call from?" Aidan asked.

"A guard at County who keeps us updated. Told me the job was done."

"What job?" Berat said.

"That's what I'm telling you, I don't know. Then Russo comes over at the gala and tells me to go with his men. That I need a reminder of who's in charge."

"Do you know Darien White?" Matt asked.

"Yeah." He took a sip from the bottle of water Rick offered, wincing as it hit his split lip. "That fucking meth head owes me fifty grand. His—" He cut himself off, hesitating.

Aidan cut a glance at the timer. "Three more minutes."

"His envelopes are always light. I figure he's skimming product for himself."

"That's not all he was skimming," Berat said. "He had an attic full of stolen electronics."

Patrick set aside the bottle and lowered his chin. "Shit."

"You didn't know?"

"No, I missed it." He dragged his good hand through his hair. "I've been so busy trying to juggle my parents and Lara's parents and keep them all from finding out she's pregnant before we can get married. Irish Catholics, Italian Catholics—they'll lose their fucking minds."

"I'm sure they can do the math," Jamie said. "Eventually."

"We'll be married by then." His blue eyes hardened. "They can all fuck off."

"So you don't know about the diamonds?" Aidan said.

Pudge's gaze whipped to him. "What fucking diamonds?"

"The multimillion dollars' worth that Darien White said he stole on *your* orders."

He shot off the table. "I will fucking murder that junkie myself."

"Too late. Your man inside already did that."

"Holy fuck." He wavered on his feet, and if not for Rick grabbing him by the good arm and lowering him into the closest chair, Jamie was sure he would've hit the deck.

"Someone's not a fan, Pudge," Rick said, claiming the chair beside him. "And they're setting you up to take the fall. Got any guesses who?"

He didn't have to think about his response. "Michael Martino," he answered instantly.

Jamie's gaze connected with Aidan's across the table. Now they were getting somewhere, everything leading back to Martino.

"Why's that?" Rick asked, continuing to play the good cop. "Why Martino?"

Pudge glanced at the clock again.

"Forty-five seconds," Matt said.

"And it better be good," Aidan pressed. "Because White said he was delivering those diamonds to Michael's dead brother for you. I don't know that I buy you two aren't working together."

"Okay, listen," Pudge said, spreading his scraped and swollen hand on the table. "After you guys popped Michael's brother, Russo didn't want anything to do with them. Neither did Lara."

"Who was she to Michael?" Berat asked.

"They were engaged."

"And now you two are together."

Pudge nodded. "As for the business, Arty and Michael had their own connections. Some of the business splintered and went Michael's way."

Matt stepped closer. "Like the jewelry theft business?"

"That, high-end financial stuff, cybercrimes. The stuff Russo wanted out of. Big bucks, sure, but a lot of attention if it goes sideways."

"Any idea what Martino's playing at now?" Aidan asked.

"Revenge," Pudge offered. "Set me and Russo up so he can take the rest of the business too."

"And get his girl back."

The buzzer sounded, but not as loudly as Pudge's conviction, his gaze hardening once more. "That's never gonna happen."

"Then tell us where Martino might be."

"There a hockey game in town?"

"Tomorrow night," Berat said.

"He'll be there."

Jamie flashed Aidan a grin. "Guess you're going back to that arena after all."

TWENTY-SIX

Aidan finished his call with Matt, then rotated against the balcony rail, watching the happy family inside decorate the Christmas tree.

Bev and Izzy stringing twinkling multicolor lights.

Angel, exaggerated mutiny on his face, holding a box of orange and black Giants ornaments in one hand, blue and gold Warriors ones in the other.

Jamie claiming innocence, genuinely surprised—Aidan had slipped the ornaments into the order—and no one buying it.

Especially when Maryanne, Izzy's friend they'd invited over, held up a matching box of light blue and white Tar Heel baubles, an ode to Jamie's alma matter that Aidan had likewise added to the order cart.

Jamie turned, searching for him, and met his gaze through the glass door. *You set me up,* he mouthed around a grin.

Aidan gave him a *Who, me?* shrug before turning back to the water. He rested his forearms on the rail, staring out at the ocean, the setting sun a beautiful sight like the one inside but not nearly so painful.

He wasn't surprised when the balcony door slid open a few minutes later. His husband knew him better than anyone. Big warm hands spanned his lower back, then slid up and around his middle, lifting his arms off the rail so Jamie could embrace him from behind.

Aidan rested back against Jamie, giving him some of his weight, Jamie strong enough in every sense to take it. "You told me not to let you do this."

Aidan closed his eyes and angled his face, nuzzling Jamie's jaw. "Do what?"

"Push us away."

A harsh chuckle escaped his lips as Aidan let his head fall back against Jamie's shoulder.

"What?" Jamie said, squeezing his middle.

"It was *you* then. Don't push *you* away. Now it's *us*." Fuck, how had so much changed in only five days? The case part Aidan could grasp, could throw himself into, but this part his mind and heart were having a hard time comprehending.

"What did Matt have to say?" Jamie asked, throwing him that rope, offering Aidan a chance to steady himself with case talk before they discussed the hard stuff.

"We're all set. Matt, Rick, and Berat are already at the arena, coordinating with security and local, and I've got our tickets in my email." Once they'd confirmed Martino's club-level seats had not been resold for the game tonight, they'd spent the day prepping tactical plans. Aidan and Jamie would be several sections over with a view, and Jamie would be tapped into the comms operation Rick would run for the rest of the tactical teams scattered about the arena and at the nearest exits. Their plan was to observe first—see if Martino met with anyone of interest—then take him discreetly into custody. The end of game crowd clearing out of the arena would be a workable opportunity, but Aidan hoped they would get the chance sooner, when less innocents were in the way.

Laughter behind them drew his gaze around Jamie's shoulder. Izzy and Maryanne were playfully refereeing a standoff between the kids, Angel after the bowl of popcorn that Bev was using to create strings for the tree.

"Good idea to invite Maryanne over," Jamie said.

"Izzy needed some company besides the kids." He righted himself in Jamie's arms, back to his front again. "And even if this is over tonight, I want to know they're safe at her party, especially if we're . . ." The words deserted him, caught behind a lump in his throat.

"If we're back home."

"Five days, Whiskey," he said, shaking his head, still unable to wrap his mind around the current state of things.

Jamie held him tighter and pressed his lips to his temple. "Talk to me, Irish."

The complete safety Aidan felt in his arms made the hard words—their ramifications—a little easier to say. "We have so much family already, but this feels . . ." He swallowed hard, forcing down that lump, then said the scary part out loud. "This feels like ours, Jamie."

"It does." Jamie's smile curved against his cheek. "You Talleys really do like to pick up strays."

He chuckled, remembering how Mel, Nic, and Cam had once called themselves that—strays. How Jamie had too. Then sobered at recalling what Marsh had said just the other day, about family falling into your lap sometimes.

Except there was a critical difference in Aidan's case; the truth he couldn't assuage with Christmas trees, silly ornaments, or all the colcannon in the world.

"Can I, though," he said, voice scratchy, "if I made them that way?"

"Oh, baby."

"I know it was Tom's and Gabe's decisions," he said as he turned in Jamie's arms. "But I feel like I'm taking something that doesn't belong to me."

"One, you're not taking anything." He covered Aidan's hands where they rested on his chest, over the tattoo where they were always drawn to. "We can only give *if* they want to take from us. And two, you had nothing to do with Bev's situation. If not for Angel in her life, which brought you into her life, she might still be in that closet in Deidra White's house."

As if on cue, Bev's "Victory!" sounded from inside, followed by cheers and laughter, and Angel's "Cheater!"

Aidan was both flying and sinking, both joyful and wretched. "We can't take her from them, though." She needed Angel and Izzy, and Angel and Izzy needed her, and there were people in San Francisco that needed him and Jamie, and he and Jamie needed them too. And that was even assuming Bev would want to stay with them, or with Izzy, after this was all over, let alone if social services would let her.

Jamie must have recognized the mental and emotional dizziness threatening to overwhelm him. He snaked an arm around his shoulders and pulled him close again. "We'll work it out. Like we always do."

"I want this, Jamie. If they'll have us, I want them in our lives, including Bev."

Jamie's laughter surprised him into glancing up to the baby blues that were full of the love Aidan had come to depend on. "In all the years I've known you, Aidan Talley, you always get what you want." One side of his smile hitched higher, into a smirk. "Even if at first you refuse to admit it's what you actually want."

Like Aidan had refused to admit he wanted Jamie, that he'd been falling for his new partner. "I admitted it."

"Eventually," Jamie added, before stealing his lips in a kiss that reminded Aidan of the kiss they'd shared on a balcony in Galveston. Jamie comforting him as fate had rushed up to meet Aidan when he'd least expected it.

The balcony door swooshed opened. "I need a tall person," Bev interrupted. "Either of you will do."

Aidan just laughed, his forehead falling against Jamie's shoulder.

Fate.

Right in your lap, he mentally heard Marsh remark, smirk and all.

"What about both of us?" Jamie said to Bev as he carded his fingers through Aidan's hair, centering him the way no one else could.

"That'll work too."

Righting his head, Aidan took a deep breath and clasped Jamie's hand, ready to meet fate with his partner. "What's the mission?" he asked Bev.

"Put this on the top of the tree." She handed him a tree topper that was a red, white, and blue star with the C hugging LA logo in the middle.

Aidan laughed out loud. "Where did you find this?"

"Convenience store where Ward took us to get the

popcorn and string. It's the team he plays for, right? The guy whose place we're borrowing?"

"It is," Jamie said, fighting his own laughter.

"Well, he should have at least one ornament for his team on the tree." She shoved the star at Jamie. "It can keep the peace among the others."

Jamie finally lost the battle, laughing so hard he was practically wheezing.

"What?" Bev said. "I pay zero attention to sports, so help me out here."

"I don't think anyone has ever referred to that team as peacekeepers."

She threw her hands up. "I was just trying for a compromise team. We're all gonna have to get behind one if this is ever gonna work." She spun on her heel, heading back inside, leaving Aidan with one hand in Jamie's and the other holding the last symbol of his future he would've ever imagined.

"Nic will fucking kill you," Jamie snickered. "At least convince her to go with Sacto so he's got someone to watch games with."

"I'll work on it," Aidan said with a smile. Jamie started forward to follow Bev inside, but Aidan tugged him back. He waited for Jamie's gaze before asking, "Do you want this too?" He was pretty sure he knew the answer, but he needed to be sure Jamie was on board with all this, because Jamie would always be his top priority too.

Jamie's answering smile was almost as beautiful as the one from their wedding day. "The only thing I've ever wanted more is you, Irish."

TWENTY-SEVEN

"View's a bit different from up here," Jamie said as he and Aidan took their seats at the end of a row around the bowl from Martino's suite. They had a good view of their suspect's intended location—and of the rink, which Jamie had only ever seen as a court before, from the sidelines most recently. The bigger, different picture wasn't bad.

Beside him, Aidan cursed and adjusted the hat he wasn't used to wearing. Jamie could count on one hand the number of times over the last eight years he'd seen his husband in a ballcap. But sitting as close as they were to Martino, Aidan's red hair would be too noticeable. Ditto Jamie—all of him—so he'd also donned a hat and, God help him, the black and silver of the hometown team, hoping to blend in and avoid a cameraman spotting him and putting him on the scoreboard.

Aidan left his own hat alone and adjusted Jamie's lower. "How much is it killing you to wear that gear?"

"Almost more than my Carolina heart can bear. I'd rather be in red tonight. What about you?"

Aidan shrugged. "I have no real hockey allegiances. I'd just rather attend sporting events where I don't freeze my nuts off."

Jamie slung an arm around his shoulders and drew him closer. "I'll keep you warm, baby." And this close, it was easy for Jamie to hold his phone in his lap and show Aidan the live feed from inside Martino's box, streaming to them from the surveillance bug the advance teams had placed.

Aidan rubbed his ear, activating the comm unit there. "We're reading," he told Matt and Rick, who were set up in a nearby concession stand that had been closed for the evening. "Nice work."

"Now let's just hope he shows," Jamie mumbled, eyeing the empty suite. It was fully stocked—trays of snacks and buckets of beer ready to go—but not a single guest in sight. Yet.

A text appeared at the top of Jamie's phone screen, Angel pinging him with another question about mods to the truck.

Aidan rubbed his ear again. "That was a genius move," he said with a jut of his chin at Jamie's text thread with Angel.

"You're the one who told me about his interest after the chase and about Tom's history with cars. And you've been pretty good with Bev yourself."

"She's a cool kid and not a kid at all. What she's been through . . ."

"That's over for her now, one way or the other." He texted Angel back one-handed with a suggested tweak to his proposed mod, then asked, **Everything good there?**

A picture appeared, Jamie's tablet in the foreground, Angel sitting at the table with it, while Izzy, Bev, and

Maryanne were in the living room watching a rom-com Jamie recalled seeing previews for. **Make it stop**, read Angel's message with the picture.

With any luck, you're back to school tomorrow. Enjoy the night off while you still can.

He responded with the crying face emoji, at which point Aidan snagged the phone from Jamie and recorded a voice message, in Spanish, telling Angel he couldn't afford to miss any more Spanish lessons.

Vete a la mierda came right back.

Aidan bit out a laugh as he handed the phone back to Jamie, but beneath the amusement, Jamie could see him struggling. The shake of his hand, the gleam in his eyes, the hope that vibrated under his skin. How much he enjoyed getting to know Angel and Izzy again, Bev too, and how much he wanted it to all work out so they could stay in one another's lives. Jamie wanted that too, wanted Aidan happy most of all.

He put the phone in the cupholder where they could both see it, then hauled Aidan as close as the armrest between them allowed, his lips pressed against Aidan's temple just below the brim of his hat. "It's okay, Irish. I've got you."

They stayed seated close until player introductions and the anthem, and when they sat back down, it was to motion in Martino's box, finally. Martino was in attendance, dressed in jeans and a black team-branded sweater. Two other people were in the box with him. One a hired guard if Jamie had to guess, the overly muscled, younger man hanging back, while Martino chatted with a suited gentleman closer to the front of the box.

Aidan swiped a hand over his ear, Jamie over his too,

the both of them activating their comms just as Rick reported, "We've got eyes on."

No ears on tonight, audio surveillance beyond what they could legally do with so many other people in range and beyond what would be useful with so much background noise, as evidenced by the cheer that went up at the opening face-off.

"ID on the current visitor?" Aidan asked.

"Luca Savoy," Rick answered so fast he couldn't have used facial recognition for it. "Former hockey player. Broadcaster now."

"Someone else is a fan," Jamie said.

"Lotta frozen-over lakes in the Midwest during the winter," Rick replied. "Shit for balance on blades, though, so I watched a lot more than I ever played."

Savoy wasn't the only former athlete to visit Martino during the first period. Martino's suite saw a steady stream of comings and goings, the snacks and drinks requiring multiple refills. Some of the faces Jamie recognized—more athletes, some celebrities—others he didn't but could guess at their business. "You getting good enough looks for facial?" he asked the team.

"Most of them," Rick replied. "Everyone we've run so far is either a celebrity, athlete, or criminal with a rap sheet."

"Some are two or more of those things," Matt deadpanned.

"Starting to wonder about this one in particular," Berat chimed in from his spot at the bowl's entrance closest to Martino's suite. "Incoming."

On cue, a new visitor appeared on screen, one Jamie recalled from last night. And from last summer. Same as both those times, he was dressed all in black again, from his hair, to his leather jacket and jeans, to the bracelets on his wrists and the rings on his fingers.

Aidan seemed to recognize him too. "He was at the party last night, wasn't he? Who is he?"

"Ryan Lassiter," Jamie answered. "He's in some band all the kids love." Aidan's brows raced north, colliding with the cap's rim. Understandably so, Jamie more the movie kind of guy, Aidan the music one, but Aidan's tastes veered toward Irish punk, not the latest rock-pop sensation. "They're Levi's son's favorite. We ran into Ryan when questioning a suspect on the case for Press this past summer."

"A case that also involved cargo thefts. And now we're running into him again, last night with Russo, tonight with Martino, on another stolen goods case."

"Doesn't look like he's here with good news for Martino either," Rick said.

"If I had to bet money," Aidan speculated, "I'd guess it's a message from Russo."

As the rock star towered over Martino, in his face about something, Jamie had to agree with their assessments. "Matt, you know anything more?" Jamie asked, recalling some nonverbal sparks flying between him and Ryan the last time they'd run into him. *Bedroom eyes*, Marsh had teased.

There was nothing funny, however, about Matt's tone when he reentered the conversation, his timbre low and strained. "What the fuck is he doing here?" His gruff question was followed by his comm disconnecting, then Rick's "Matt, where are you going?"

"Berat," Aidan said, "Be ready to intercept if he's headed your way."

"I don't think he'll do that," Rick said. "Not in his interest."

"What's that mean?"

"You remember the guy last night, at the bar?"

"Matt's brother," Jamie said.

"Yeah, that was him. He's in the band with Ryan."

Another detail clicked. "That's why the place was called Remedy."

"Vice versa, but not the point. Matt's . . . protective . . . of his brother."

"The rock star?" Aidan said.

And another detail registered for Jamie, but not knowing how much of his personal life Matt had or wanted disclosed, he signaled Aidan to go off comms.

"What do you know?" Aidan asked, immediately catching on.

"Matt and Cam worked together in Boston because they had something in common. His sibling was missing too for some time, and while he came back, he wasn't the same. Matt's been trying for years to reconnect with him. Probably part of the reason he moved out west, then up to LA."

"And he doesn't want Ryan to fuck that up."

"That'd be my guess." And maybe they had in fact all misread Matt's reaction to Ryan this past summer. Jamie scratched a mental note to apologize, then clicked his comm back on when Aidan did.

"Update, Berat?" Aidan requested.

"No sign of Matt down here," the detective reported.

"And looks like Ryan is leaving Martino's suite," Jamie said, watching on his phone screen as the rock star stormed out of the suite.

"Whatever was said," Aidan remarked, "Martino's

going about business as usual." Proven as he guzzled the rest of his beer, plastered on a smile, and greeted the next visitor who entered the suite. "Does this guy even need to get rid of Russo?" Aidan said. "Seems like he's got plenty of business and connections."

"We're still missing something," Jamie said. "A connection."

"Ryan?"

"I don't think that's it. He's just a messenger. And consistent with everything else we've seen tonight already."

But the visitor who entered the suite next was not. He looked like an average guy just off the street, a little younger than Jamie, about Aidan's height, his blond hair windswept, his cheeks rosy, his jeans and sweatshirt fan appropriate. But the way Martino greeted him was warmer than he'd greeted anyone else that night. A tight embrace, a kiss on the cheek, an arm slung over his shoulders as they cheered on the face-off at the start of the third period.

"Something's different about this one," Aidan likewise detected.

"Do we have a match on facial?" Jamie asked Rick, something about this latest visitor also familiar.

"Not registering on facial," Rick said.

"I'll get on the horn with ticketing," Matt said, sounding out of breath but back on the comms with them. "See if we can trace the ticket that got him in."

"Friend?" Jamie speculated while they waited.

Aidan tilted his head, as if considering his options. "More than, maybe? A boyfriend?"

"Try family," Rick said. "He wasn't a match to anyone in the system, but when I ran him against Michael, he was a match on the nose, eyes, and dimpled chin."

"But Michael doesn't have kids," Aidan said. "Neither did Arthur."

"What about other siblings?" Jamie asked. "Kids, maybe?"

Aidan shook his head. "No other siblings."

"I've got a name," Matt said. "Fuck."

Jamie shifted forward in his seat, same as Aidan beside him. "What is it?" Jamie asked.

"William *Arthur* Dunlap."

Aidan moved to shoot out of his seat, but Jamie threw out an arm, holding him in place. "Don't draw attention," he said. "He's not going anywhere, and we've got him covered. Let me help Rick dig and try to confirm it." Trusting Aidan to see reason, he withdrew his arm so he could have both hands to type as fast as he could on his phone, running every search he could think of on William Arthur Dunlap.

Beside him, Aidan propped his elbows on his knees and scrubbed his hands over his face. "How did we miss this? Is he actually Arthur's son?"

"There's no record of kids in Arty's existing Bureau file," Berat said. "Or in the one Sutton pulled together. When I got roped into this, I read through everything. It's not in there."

"But between the resemblance, his familiarity with Michael, and the middle name… Fuck. Angel *was* supposed to meet Arty. That part was the truth." His words grew thready as he continued to speak. "It was just the wrong Arty. His son. Fuck."

Jamie spared a hand to run over his shoulders. "Breathe, Irish."

"We were the missing link. Me and Tom. It's revenge. Just not the revenge we thought."

"You take his father," Matt said. "He takes your godson."

"Or you from your godson," Berat offered a most unpleasant alternative. "Timing just happened to be when you were in town . . ."

"I've got his birth certificate," Jamie said, the document loading on his screen. "Mother was Jill Dunlap. No father listed. Looks like there was a second certificate but it's under seal. A twin that was adopted, maybe? Give me a second." He typed faster, digging deeper, putting every hacker skill he had to use for his family, looking for that connection. When he found it, his stomach fell to the floor. It wasn't William's resemblance to his possible uncle that had struck Jamie as familiar.

Aidan clasped his biceps. "Jamie, what is it?"

"William's sister is Maryanne MacIntyre." He flipped the phone so Aidan could see the picture loading on screen. "The same Maryanne at the condo with our family."

This time, when Aidan shot to the end of his seat and out of it, Jamie didn't stop him. Instead, he was right on his heels. Charging for the exits and their family.

TWENTY-EIGHT

Aidan had never been so glad that he'd married someone with a lead foot as he was tonight. The escort Berat called in for them helped too, the two cruisers cutting a path with lights and sirens, cutting the time from downtown to Manhattan Beach by half.

Still not fast enough, as Aidan took the stairs to the condo two at a time, heart in his throat. Ward was waiting at the door for them. "They're all still fine," he said, same as he had over the phone. "All asleep. I just checked. Every five minutes like you asked."

"Thank you," Aidan said before sprinting inside, needing to lay eyes on them himself.

Jamie hung back, asking Ward questions like what time Maryanne had left and if he'd noticed anything off, then reporting it to Berat, Matt, and Rick, who were scattering teams to surveil William and Martino post-game. They wouldn't be moving on anyone tonight, not until they got a better picture of the totality of what they were dealing with.

And not until Aidan saw for himself that the family he wanted to keep was safe.

The teen curled up on the sleeper sofa in the upstairs loft, Jamie's tablet propped on his pillow, Angel having fallen asleep working on that truck.

The other teen soundly asleep in one guest bedroom, covers pulled up tight to her chin.

His childhood best friend, standing in the doorway of the other guest room, a mix of worry and hope on her face. "Is it over already?"

Aidan crossed the loft in three long strides and hauled Izzy, safe and sound, into his arms. "Oh, thank fuck." It was a struggle not to let it all go right there, but that would only upset Izzy, and that wasn't what he wanted. He just needed to convince his brain that they were all okay. That they were safe. That fate hadn't yet pulled a cruel trick and snatched away the family it had just dropped in his life.

Izzy wrapped her arms around him, a hand coasting up and down his back. "Hey, what's going on, cariño?"

He smiled, remembering how she used to call him that as kids whenever his teenage Irish temper would get the better of him. Or when he was struggling with being the different one with the dyed hair and funny accent. She'd always been there with a gentle word and the patience he'd needed from a peer.

From a friend.

He drew back and lightly clasped her shoulder. "You're okay? And the kids?"

"Yeah, we're fine. Maryanne left after we finished the movie. They"—she nodded in the direction of the kids—"fell asleep before it was over. I was reading, but I guess I fell asleep too."

Jamie appeared at the top of the stairs. "All good?"

Aidan nodded, but same as him, Jamie needed to make his own checks too. First on Angel, also collecting his tablet as he circled the sleeper, then he skirted around the other couch and chairs to check on Bev, poking a head in the guest room to make sure she was okay, then gently pulling her door shut.

"What's going on?" Izzy said as Jamie rejoined them. "You're back way earlier than I remember stakeouts going, and you both look like you've been through hell."

"Let's discuss downstairs," Jamie said, then led them that way, to the dining table.

"What's going on?" Izzy asked again once they were settled.

"We just need to make sure—" Aidan started.

Only to be cut off by Izzy's uncompromising "No. The days of you shielding me from shit are over. I do not have the time or energy for that. None of us do. Tell me." He remembered that tone too, from when they were kids and she wouldn't put up with his bullshit. Remembered the worst extreme of it the day she'd cut him out of her and Angel's lives. She didn't deserve to be in the dark then, and she didn't now.

"Okay, I'll tell you what I can." At her nod, he continued. "Tom and I worked a case about ten years ago. We put someone in jail. A mob fence."

"That's the person who resells stolen goods?"

"That's right."

"What happened to him?"

"He died there."

"So then he's not the one behind this."

"Not exactly." Aidan raked a hand through his hair, still

cursing himself for not making the connections sooner, for totally missing this a decade ago. "We just learned today that he may have had two children. That's who we think targeted Angel. Who targeted me."

"Do you know who they are? And are they mob?"

"They're not," Jamie said. "At least we don't think they are, but their uncle is, like their dad was."

"Their uncle?"

"A man named Michael."

Izzy froze, and all of the color bled from her light brown face. She covered her gaping mouth with a hand. "Oh no . . ."

Aidan covered the one that still rested on the table. "What is it?"

"Maryanne," she said. "She recently connected with her uncle, Michael. He told her he had money for her from her real father."

"Was that before she befriended you?"

"Oh god," Izzy groaned. "I'm gonna be sick."

Aidan squeezed her hand. "Just breathe, Izzy. You didn't know. None of us did."

Her gaze wandered upstairs, to the kids, then to the living room. "She was in the house here with us. She's been around Angel dozens of times."

"Which was probably how she knew he could drive," Jamie said. "How she helped her brother and uncle set him up."

"Exactly when I was in town," Aidan said. "I'm so sorry, Izzy."

She shook her head and squeezed his hand back, hard. "This is on her, not you. She and her brother tried to kill my son."

"She didn't succeed."

"Because his godfather is a smart man." She reached out her other hand, taking Jamie's. "And so is his husband. So you two geniuses tell me this—how the fuck are we going to stop them? Because I need this to be over. Now."

TWENTY-NINE

"I don't like this," Aidan said on this ninth—tenth—loop around the loft area.

"I don't like it either," Jamie said. "But we have an invite to the party at Maryanne's house, we'll have teams on us there, and the kids will have a team on them here."

"We'll keep them safe, Aidan," Mel said from where she sat across from Jamie on the other couch.

"And even though she is more than capable of doing so," said the blond Madigan in head-to-toe leather beside Mel, "I'll also make sure of it. Teenagers are kind of my specialty now. I am the best stepmom to ever stepmom."

"I'm not worried about the teenagers," Aidan said. "I'm worried about the mobsters."

Helena threw her head back and laughed, the bright sound a sharp contrast to what Aidan knew of the assassin queen's skills with blades and other sharp objects. "Oh, my dear sweet FBI man, you have so much to learn."

Aidan changed tactics, still trying to talk himself out of the plan they had spent all day nailing down with Matt,

Rick, and Berat, who were at the office putting said plan into action on the law enforcement side. "I'd rather Izzy not be there." He turned his gaze on Jamie. "Or you."

"I'm going," Jamie said. Aidan opened his mouth to no doubt protest, and Jamie kept talking, not giving him a chance. "They don't know we're on to them yet. Assuming William or Michael are planning to move on Angel and Bev, they need to *think* protection is short-staffed."

They'd been careful when bringing Mel and Danny and Helena and Celia in today. The two couples had arrived at separate times, dropped off by nondescript rideshare vehicles via the underground garage. And they'd likewise been careful to avoid the balcony where they could be surveilled, staying inside and meeting up here in the loft.

"Martino and William will expect Maryanne to report in that me, you, and Izzy are at the party." Jamie flicked his gaze toward the rail, toward the area below where Izzy sat at the dining table with Danny and Bev, who were comparing accents, and Angel and Celia, Helena's wife, who were going over truck mods. "As for Izzy, do you want to tell her to sit this one out? Because I sure as hell don't. And if you do try to tell her that, you might be the one not making it to the party tonight."

That stopped Aidan in his tracks, and he hung his head back on a heavy sigh. He knew Jamie was right. Battle won, Jamie held out a hand that Aidan finally took, letting Jamie draw him down onto the couch beside him. "Fine, y'all win," Aidan said, resignation in his grumbled acceptance. "Let's go over this one more time."

Jamie squeezed his knee, then launched into the plan detail for the umpteenth time that afternoon. Giving Aidan what he needed. "We go to the party with Izzy," Jamie said.

"We let Maryanne report that we're there, then we isolate her from the rest of the party crowd, reveal that we know who she is and what she's playing at, and we extract a confession. Then we turn her over to the backup team there."

"And William?"

"If he's at the party, then we isolate him next. Same procedure."

"And if he's here instead," Mel said, "then we take down him and Martino. Question William first, as he's more likely to confess."

"In either case," Jamie said, "we already have charges against Martino for hacking TE, orchestrating the cargo thefts, and for issuing the kill order on White." While it had appeared the email to Russo's inmate who'd done the deed had come from Pudge on Russo's orders, it had in fact been a spoofed email address and message that Jamie traced back to the same IP address that had hacked into TE. To Michael Martino.

"Do we expect interference from the other half of the Mafia equation?" Helena asked. Keeping the actual case details light, they'd focused their earlier brief to her on the parties involved, most of whom she was already familiar with. None of them would be happy to find the Madigans involved; more firepower for his and Jamie's team.

"Russo wants no part of it," Aidan said. "That was the message to Martino at the game yesterday. Same was relayed to Matt by Russo's messenger. Russo's pissed this was made to look like him. Not the kind of business or attention he wants."

"So no Mafia back up?"

"Not from Russo, but Martino had muscle with him at the game."

"And he's got a profitable, high-end operation going," Jamie said. "He's got more firepower in his pocket too."

"Except this particular matter is personal for him," Mel said. "He wants revenge for his brother. He'll be here or there to handle it himself."

That was the consensus they'd all reached that afternoon. Which only made Aidan's knee bounce faster under Jamie's hand. He squeezed it again. "We should have them outnumbered," Jamie said. "Two teams on us, two teams on the condo, plus Mel and Helena inside here."

"And we're also invested," Helena added. "Our partners are here too."

"We'll stay in touch throughout, Aidan," Mel assured him. "You'll know every step of the way what's going on here."

Aidan raked a hand through his hair, and when he spoke again, it was raspy, the words ragged, like his emotions. "Mel, this—"

"I know, hermano. We can't afford to lose more family, especially not the ones we just got back. I won't let it happen."

A throat cleared to their right, Izzy at the top of the stairs. "Can you give us a moment?" she said to Mel and Helena.

"Of course," Mel said as they rose, Jamie rising to go with them.

"Can you stay?" Izzy said to him. "This affects you too."

Jamie sank back into the couch beside Aidan, and Izzy settled into the chair Helena had been sitting in on Aidan's other side.

She took a deep breath, licked her lips, nervous about whatever she had to say. And when she started, there was a sheen in her eyes, and her voice was as scratchy as Aidan's had been earlier.

Aidan reached out a hand to her. "Izzy, we don't have to—"

"Yeah, we do," she said, as she took his hand. "This needs to be over. We need our lives back." She sniffled, then charged ahead, the same determination and bravery on display that Aidan had witnessed in her all week. "If God forbid anything happens to me, you're his guardian. I never changed that in the will."

Aidan was glad he was sitting, otherwise his knees would've given out. "Izzy."

"Is that okay with you?" she asked Aidan.

"You know it is, but I have no intention of letting that come to pass."

She looked to Jamie. "Same question."

"One hundred percent," he answered without hesitation. "Including to what Aidan said. We will do everything in our power to make sure nothing happens to any of you."

"Including him?" she said with a nod toward Aidan.

Jamie's bright blue eyes locked on him, and Aidan hoped like hell Jamie saw in his own gaze all the love and gratitude Aidan felt for him. "He's the best thing that ever happened to me," Jamie told them both. "And this week, as wild as it has been, might be the second best of my life, behind our wedding one. I won't let anything happen to any of you."

THIRTY

Maryanne threw open her wreathed front door, all smiles and holiday cheer. "You made it!" As her gaze skipped over Izzy's shoulder to Jamie and Aidan, a frown flitted across her face, but it vanished just as quickly. "And I didn't expect you two! You told me we were getting the green giant," she said to Izzy.

"Well, he's not Ward, but this one"—Izzy backhanded Aidan in the stomach—"is Irish, so he counts as green. And his husband here"—she backhanded Jamie with her other hand—"is a giant, so we can just add them together and call it even."

Maryanne hooted with laughter, and Jamie had to hand it to Izzy, she was quick with the puns and a pro at pretending all was normal. He'd have to ask her sometime if that came naturally or if it was a side effect of dealing with unruly airline passengers.

"That works for me," Maryanne said once her hilarity subsided. She opened the door wider for them to enter. "No Angel and Bev?"

"We needed an adult's night, and they needed a no adults one."

They handed their jackets to Maryanne, who hung them on top of the other coats on the hooks by the door. Counting jackets, Jamie confirmed the small but decent crowd Matt and Rick had already reported to them through their comms, surveilling as they were from a nearby location with sight lines.

"Fair enough," Maryanne said as she led them down a hallway toward the back of the house, holiday music and muted voices drifting in from the same direction. They emerged into an open kitchen and dining area, bottles of wine and charcuterie trays arranged on the table, a gathering of folks milling around on the patio outside, clustered near the outdoor heaters. "Please help yourselves," Maryanne said. "I'm just going to go check the garage fridge for more cheese and meat."

"Can I help with anything?" Izzy asked.

"No, I'm good." Her smile didn't quite reach her eyes, and if Jamie didn't know better, he'd think some part of her regretted what she was about to do. "Enjoy your kid-free evening."

She slipped out the side door, and Jamie reported in through his comm. "Maryanne's making the call."

"No movement at the condo," Berat relayed.

"Kids?" Izzy asked.

"All good," Jamie assured her. "No movement there. You want a glass of wine?"

"Please," she said, the show on pause as she white-knuckled the edge of the island, her arms spread. "Red."

He grabbed a bottle off the table and poured a glass at the island, all the while mentally counting the seconds

Maryanne remained outside. "We just gonna wait here for her?" he asked Aidan. "Or go out there?"

"Give her fifteen more seconds."

"She's not coming back."

They whipped around toward the new voice, and Jamie's pulse ratcheted up another notch. Michael Martino stood at the hallway opening, dressed in a black sweater and slacks, hands in his pockets, shoulder leaned against the wall.

At the same time, Matt radioed, "Looks like the party is breaking up."

Or had never been a real party to start. Jamie peeked out the sliding glass door and pretended to be confused by what he was seeing. "Where's everyone going, Martino?" he asked, letting their teams know Michael was on-site, likely smuggled in the same way they'd smuggled in their own backup. They'd known it was a possibility.

"Gave 'em the rest of the night off," Martino said.

"Hired some actors, did you?" Aidan said, dispensing with the cover since it seemed Martino was too.

"This is LA. Plenty of 'em."

"Garage door is opening," Matt relayed.

Aidan moved at the same time Jamie did, stepping closer so they formed a wall between Izzy and Martino and so the island was at their backs, not the garage door where Martino's muscle might enter.

"Sounds like the garage door's going up," Aidan said, not letting on that they were miked up. "Where's Maryanne going? We still want to talk to her."

"We've got a team on her," Rick said, correctly interpreting the order Aidan was also giving them.

"Is William with her?" Jamie asked.

"Negative," Rick said. "She's alone."

"No," Martino answered as well. "He's on a different mission."

"To go after my kid?" Izzy said, pushing her way through Jamie and Aidan's wall. "Again? Don't you think almost ruining his life once was enough?"

As angry as she was, Martino was cool and calm, almost bored. His placid demeanor worried Jamie; he either had more backup nearby or didn't care which way this face-off went. Not good for them either way.

"They weren't much older than your son when this one" —he jutted his chin at Aidan—"and your husband locked up their dad. My brother. Sentenced him to death."

"We wouldn't have had to lock him up," Aidan said, "if he hadn't been fencing goods for the mob."

"He didn't deserve to go to jail for that. Orlando Russo did."

"Is that why you tried to frame him for the cargo thefts against TE?" Jamie asked. "Then for White's murder?"

"If I could take him down too, worth it."

Too. Meaning Russo was one—but not the only one—of Martino's targets.

"So what?" Aidan said. "You've got William going after Russo and Maryanne after Angel? Or vice versa?"

"They know what they have to do."

"Ryan, it's Matthew," Jamie overheard Matt through the comm. "Martino has someone coming after Russo. I'm sending you pictures now."

"But what if we knew what you were going to do?" Aidan asked the mobster in the room with them. "If we'd already figured out who William and Maryanne were to you and Arty?" Jamie recognized Aidan's even tone as a poke, not a boast. He was trying to assess exactly what Martino was after, exactly how far he'd go.

Not a flinch.

Jamie's heart raced faster, and when he caught Aidan's gaze, the same concern shone in his eyes. They were dealing with a loose cannon driven solely by revenge.

Without an exit plan.

Fuck.

"Guess that makes you smarter than me," Martino said with a shrug.

"What *was* the plan?" Aidan asked as he maneuvered next to Jamie again, Izzy behind them, and shifting so they were a step closer to the patio door. "This can only end one way: with you caught."

"I have a better idea." Michael pushed off the door and withdrew a lighter from his pocket. "All of you pay the price for taking Arty from us."

Confirming Aidan was also one of those other targets, as they'd suspected.

And he and Izzy were in the blast radius.

Because if Jamie figured right, this house was about the same age as Aidan's old one in Redwood City. Meaning it likely ran on natural gas—the pilot light, water heater, and heating unit in the attached garage that Maryanne had just gone out of. If she'd released gas into the house or there'd been carbon monoxide already, they wouldn't smell it. But that lighter in Martino's hand, when flicked, would ignite it.

Fuck. Fuck!

Aidan must have made the same calculation when he'd started moving them toward the patio door.

They made another step in that direction, and Jamie

asked a different question, buying them more time to reach the exit. "So was it ever about Angel? Other than to lure Aidan into this?"

"Oh, I planned to make you feel the loss of the kids too, including the girl you two have gotten so attached to. But Russo sent his pet rock star and said they were off-limits. Under his protection. Fine, they can feel the loss of all of you. Means I don't have to drag this out any longer."

"Including your own life?" Aidan said. "Because if you flick that lighter and there's gas in this house, it all goes boom, with you in it too."

"I'm a dead man anyway. Rock star told me that too. So I made the arrangements I needed to. William and Maryanne will be taken care of. Nothing left to do now but avenge my brother."

There'd be no talking Martino out of this, no negotiating, no bringing him in. He was determined to die and take Aidan and Izzy with him. And Jamie promised to do anything to protect his family.

So when Martino flipped open the top of the lighter and moved his thumb over the spark wheel, Jamie didn't hesitate. Grabbing the closest wine bottle, he chucked it as hard as he could in Martino's direction, distracting him the precious few seconds Aidan needed to wrench the patio door open, before the blast hurtled them the rest of the way out of it.

THIRTY-ONE

Jamie hated to think how much money Danny had thrown around to get the nurses to allow this many people at this time of night into Aidan's hospital room. Granted, it was closer to dawn than dusk, closer to visiting hours than from them, but they were still outside the designated hours, and Jamie was fairly certain the four of them inside the room and the even larger group of people waiting in the hall were far outside the maximum number of visitors.

Especially when the patient was still unconscious.

Jamie glanced again at the heart monitor beside Aidan's bed. Strong and steady. Same as Aidan's breaths, unassisted by any machines. And his hand in Jamie's was warm, evidence of the life and blood that still coursed through his husband's body.

Immediately after the blast, once Jamie and Izzy had dug themselves out from the blast rubble around them, Jamie had suffered a panic-inducing, heart-sickening few minutes during which he first couldn't find Aidan, and then when he had, thinking he had lost him for good. With

Aidan's limp and seemingly lifeless body in his arms, Jamie could've sworn his own heart stopped. That with the center of his world gone, there would be no going on for him either. But then Izzy had appeared beside him, had grabbed his chin, and forced him to focus. Aidan was alive and needed their help. He'd followed her orders as she'd checked Aidan's vitals and administered the first aid she'd been taught as a flight attendant, taking care of him until the paramedics had arrived. Once at the hospital, they'd been briefly separated, he and Izzy checked for concussions and any injuries other than the obvious scrapes and bruises, while Aidan had been wheeled back for X-rays and scans.

According to the doctors, he'd taken a hit, from the roof and the ground, and his brain wasn't happy about it. No bleeds but some swelling that should recede. And he should wake up, they'd assured him.

Should. Not a definitive would.

"Aidan told me about a time you got injured," Angel said from the chair beside him, cutting off the spiral Jamie's mind was about to go down again. "That he wouldn't leave your bedside."

"That's right." A fire and blast that had been multitudes bigger than the one last night had knocked Jamie unconscious, and after being trapped under a ceiling beam and suffering smoke inhalation prior to that, he'd been severely compromised, his body and mind taking a while to come back online. When he woke, it had been to Aidan's lovely red hair. And then to his hurt and anger. "He stayed until I woke, even after I'd spent months lying to him."

"He forgave you?"

Jamie wriggled his left hand, the emeralds in the titanium band around his left ring finger catching the lights overhead. "Eventually. But he was angry at first, justifiably so. We took some time apart. But we still loved each other too much to let go."

Angel's gaze bounced from Aidan, to his mother asleep in the corner lounger, then back to Aidan. "What if Mom and I took too long?"

Keeping one hand around Aidan's, he slung his other arm around Angel's shoulder, giving him a sideways hug. "You took the time you needed. Both of you."

"And I just found you two," Bev said from across the bed where she held Aidan's other hand. "So I can't see how losing Aidan now would be fair. I haven't been with you long enough to get angry and run away. I mean, I'm sure I will at some point, but not yet."

"Noted," Jamie said with a laugh, the spark of joy her words brought undeniable, hope chasing away some of the chill and the doubt that still lingered, despite the doctors' assurances.

"We won't let him go either," Angel said as he rested more fully against Jamie. He was lightly snoring in five minutes, and Jamie must have been too shortly after, because when he woke, it was to pressure around his hand and sunlight streaming in through the window across the room.

Wait.

Pressure around his hand.

He glanced up toward the head of Aidan's hospital bed and found autumn eyes watching him. "Good morning," his husband rasped.

"Oh, thank god," Jamie sighed. Carefully extricating himself from a still sleeping Angel, he rose from the chair and leaned over the bed, brushing his lips against Aidan's. "I was so fucking scared I'd lost you."

Aidan lifted their joined hands so the backs of Aidan's bandaged knuckles rubbed over his pec, where Jamie's tattoo and heart were beneath his shirt. "You can't lose me, Whiskey. I'm right here, always."

"I like you right here," Jamie said, palming his cheek. "With us."

"Us?"

He shifted so Aidan could see more fully around the room, past Angel in the chair beside Jamie's to where Izzy and Bev were curled up in the lounger. "They were scared too, but they wouldn't let you go. None of us would."

Aidan's hand clenched around his. "I'm never letting any of you again either."

THIRTY-TWO

Aidan entered the conference room on Sunday morning to cheers he didn't think he deserved. "Don't clap for me," he said, then jutted a thumb at Jamie who entered behind him. "He was the one who pushed us outside in time."

"You're still standing, Irish," Jamie said, a hand at his lower back. "That counts as an applause-worthy win. Especially on this case."

"Which we closed," Rick said. "With William and Maryanne in custody."

They'd picked up the brother and sister pair at LAX, trying to hop a flight to Europe with the money Martino had paid them to lure Aidan and Angel to him. Russo had beat them out of town on a supposedly planned vacation to Italy, but as he wasn't the target of this investigation, they hadn't notified Interpol. Nor had they stopped Pudge and Lara from flying to Las Vegas a few short hours after Russo's flight had taken off. Aidan had figured he knew what for, and that Pudge figured he was on the FBI's, LAPD's, and LBPD's radars now. Maybe he'd stick to just being a rich husband and soon-to-be father. As for Martino, he had died in the blast. Another death in addition to the White siblings. Aidan couldn't help but feel a niggle of guilt that there wouldn't have been three deaths without the original one—Arty, who he and Tom had sent to prison.

As if reading his thoughts, Jamie leaned close and whispered in his ear, "You were just doing your job, then and now."

It was an inescapable part of it, which was why it was so important to get it right. And for those criminal suspects who were arrested, doubly important that the rest of the legal process was followed as well. It certainly had been for Angel. "They'll have counsel, William and Maryanne?" Aidan asked Rooster.

The prosecutor nodded.

"Good," Aidan said, then to Matt, "I'm sorry this didn't turn out to be the answer to your jewel thief case."

"Not an answer," Matt said, "but more of a lead than I've had in over a year. We'll be working through all those visitors to Martino's box. See if any of them had been looking to buy those jewels or other stolen goods in the past."

"And we know a lot more now about the cargo theft rings operating in the city," Rick said.

"Not to mention the meth dealers," Berat added. "I shared White's list from the bathroom wall with LAPD. They've made two arrests already."

Aidan shuddered, recalling that awful house, glad that neither he nor Bev ever had to go inside it again.

"What time's your flight back today?" Matt asked.

"Last one out tonight," Aidan replied. Mel and Danny had already left with the private plane, leaving Aidan and

Jamie to fly commercial, after dinner with Izzy, Angel, and Bev.

"Good. You should have plenty of time to fill out this, then." Matt dropped a stack of familiar post-case paperwork on the table in front of where Aidan stood.

Beside him, Jamie snickered. "Don't miss that."

Matt dropped a second stack in front of Jamie. "And for you, Mr. Eyewitness and consultant."

Jamie's face fell, and Aidan laughed out loud, earning an elbow to his side. He risked another one by slapping a pen on the stack as he took his own seat. "Better get going, Whiskey. I know how long it takes you to complete these."

He sank into the chair beside him, a pout on his face and in his voice. "Did Izzy have this big a stack?"

"No," Matt said. "I filled out most of it for her."

Aidan cocked a brow. "Is someone trying to get his flirt on?"

Heat hit the agent's cheeks, but he waved off the suggestion. "Nah, just trying to do a favor for a very busy mom with two kids under her roof, for now."

Aidan had used every connection he had and pulled every string he could to get Beverly placed in Izzy's care pending review of his and Jamie's adoption application. Bev didn't want to go back into the system, and none of them, Izzy included, wanted that for her either. At Izzy's, Bev would be in a safe, stable, queer-friendly home that would allow her to finish out the school year in her current district. Aidan hoped like hell that would be enough time to push through their application and for Bev to visit San Francisco to meet the rest of their family. As much as they wanted her to be a part of their family, she had to want it too. Aidan also hoped it would give him and Jamie enough time to convince Izzy and Angel to move back to the Bay Area as well.

"And I've done a favor for you two," Rooster said as he dropped another stack of paperwork between them.

Aidan leaned back his head, glancing up at the disconcertingly dressed-down prosecutor. "Please tell me by favor you mean it's mostly filled out, otherwise we are never making that flight tonight." He tipped his head toward Jamie. "I wasn't lying about this one. Take the speed he drives at and go to the opposite end of the speedometer. That's his paperwork pace."

Rooster chuckled. "Yes, these are filled out already. You just have to submit them." Aidan drew them closer, flipping through the official documents as Rooster explained. "Affidavits of support to go with your adoption application for Beverly, including ones from Angel and Bev."

Aidan whipped his gaze back up, anger tickling the back of his throat. "You questioned—"

"Your godson and future daughter cornered me in the hospital and demanded to make statements."

"That tracks," Matt muttered on his way out the door.

Beside Aidan, Jamie laid his head on his shoulder with a heavy, dramatic sigh. "We are gonna be so hosed when they join forces with Katie."

Aidan smiled, imagining the holy trinity of terror. "I can't wait."

THIRTY-THREE

Two weeks later . . .

"So, like, what am I supposed to do?" Angel shifted side to side on his feet, the giant red blooms of the potted plant he held bobbing with the movement. "The last time I was here was for his funeral."

They stood just inside the cemetery where Gabe and Tom were buried, to the side of the walkway so they weren't in the way of others coming and going. Unlike when Aidan usually visited, the cemetery was relatively bustling today, friends and family visiting their late loved ones on Christmas Eve Day. In retrospect, he probably should've brought Angel on a less busy day, but visiting Gabe on this day was his tradition, and he'd wanted to share that with Gabe's namesake. Wanted Angel to also have a chance to reconnect with his father now that some of the anger he'd held toward Tom had dissipated too.

"Do whatever you need to," Aidan said. "Talk to him. Tell him why you haven't been here. And be honest about it. Lord knows I railed at Gabe when I found out the truth.

Get it out if you need to, if it'll help you. But then also talk to him about how you're doing. At home, at school, with your friends. Just don't tell him about the high-speed car chase."

Angel backhanded him in the stomach, same as his mother was fond of doing.

"Or just enjoy the peace of this place," Aidan said, gesturing around the small cozy cemetery with its evergreens and giant tangled oaks. This time of year, the grass was green from the cool temperatures and rain, and the wintering birds sang as they hopped around the tree roots and mulch, hunting for food. "Do whatever you need to, Angel."

"And put this on there?" he said, holding up the amaryllis.

"Your mom reminded me it was his favorite this time of year."

Izzy had wanted to come with them today too, but her flight from Paris yesterday had been cancelled. She'd finagled her way onto today's Paris to SFO flight instead, arriving later this afternoon, just in time for the Talley Christmas party. As for the kids, Jamie and Angel had flown the private plane down to pick them up on Friday evening.

"You could also tell Tom about flying on a private plane."

"You know I'm ruined forever now, right?"

"Don't tell your mother that."

"Can you hire her?" he said, not missing a beat. "The English guy on the plane . . . what was his name?"

"Jeremy?"

"Yeah, him, he mentioned something about retiring

soon. So hire Mom. She loves to travel. She loves that part of her job. The passengers, not so much."

"You don't think she'd see it as charity?" Aidan loved the idea, but he didn't want the offer to push Izzy away, not after he'd just gotten her and Angel back.

"Is it?" Angel asked.

"No, it's giving her an opportunity to do what she loves without the shitty passengers." He thought about the stack of pizza boxes from their flight Friday night and amended, "Most of the time." They'd helped Jeremy off-load them, but the cabin would probably smell like meat lovers' pizza for the next month.

Angel chuckled. "Explain it to her that way. And if it gets us back here faster, that's a win, right?"

"You want to move back here?"

"There's not much for us in LA. We could use a fresh start. Or restart, I guess. And Bev and you and Jamie will be here. That's our family now."

The certainty in his voice about Bev, the hope about moving back here to be with family, warmed Aidan's insides on the chilly December day. He looped an arm around Angel's shoulders, giving him a side hug, careful of the plants they both held. "I'll talk to Mel," he said. "If she isn't on it already. Now go. I need to go deliver my present," he said, holding up the poinsettia that was Gabe's favorite.

"Can I come talk to him too?" Angel asked. "After I'm done talking with Dad."

"Of course. You remember where Tom is?"

Angel nodded and set off in that direction while Aidan headed over to the Talley plots beneath one of the cemetery's giant oak trees. He knelt first beside his older brother's grave, passing a hand over the memorial and sending his love and holiday well wishes to the brother he'd lost too young, then rotated so he was facing Gabe's final resting place. He brushed aside the green lantana branches and nestled the poinsettia at the center of the headstone.

"Happy Christmas Eve, baby," he said. "I brought you your flower."

No Jamie? Gabe teased in his head. *I like him better.*

"Jamie's at home with our soon-to-be daughter."

He could only imagine the broad smile that would stretch across his late husband's face, the happiness that would shimmer in his eyes and the joy that would infuse his words. *Tell me everything about her.*

And he did, telling Gabe about the case and about Bev. How she'd helped them solve it, how she'd helped bring Izzy and Angel back into their lives, how her moxie and spirit hadn't withered in that closet in Deidra White's house, how that same moxie and spirit had made him and Jamie laugh every time they'd talked to her over the past two weeks.

He'd just finished telling Gabe about their plans for the house when Angel approached. His eyes were shiny, his cheeks stained with tear tracks, but there was peace about the teenager that Aidan hadn't seen since reconnecting with him. Aidan offered him a hand, and he lowered onto the ground beside him, close to his side.

"I brought you another gift too," he told Gabe. "Though don't blame me for your godson's terrible Spanish."

"Really?" Angel scoffed.

"Just setting expectations."

"Should I tell him which sports teams I root for?"

"Definitely don't do that." He bumped his shoulder

against Angel's. "I told him a little about Bev. Why don't you tell him the rest?"

He started in English, but at Aidan's correction continued in Spanish. Aidan imagined Gabe's interest, and as his smile stretched impossibly wider at the man his godson was growing up to be, his own tears began to fall, streaking his cheeks even as he laughed at the stories Angel told.

Without pausing, Angel reached over and clasped his hand, and Aidan felt the pieces of his life—his family—that had been missing click firmly back into place, and with them, the future he'd thought he lost in reach.

With Jamie by his side, with Izzy and Angel in his life again, with Bev painting every day in vivid color, he was ready to take the leap.

THIRTY-FOUR

"It's a lot, I know," Jamie said. "My first time at one of these shindigs was sensory overload."

Beside him, Bev stared around the room, wide-eyed, her gaze bouncing around the Talley manor's giant living room, from one group of people to the next or to one of the several Christmas trees visible from their seat on the couch. "Like, I knew you guys were loaded, but this is . . ." She shook her head, some of the blond strands falling out of the braid Izzy had done her hair up in for tonight's party. "Just *wow*."

"It's not about that. It's about family. The Talleys—"

"The redheaded ones?"

Jamie laughed. "Mostly, yes." It was a fair assessment. "But also the folks they've picked up along the way, like me and you."

"Aidan said they were open to new folks, but . . ." She dipped her chin, but not before Jamie saw some of the hardships she'd suffered streak across her face. Although the Talleys were an open and welcoming family, Bev had experienced the opposite in foster care, including in Deidra's home, where she'd been made to feel like an afterthought, a means to an end. That would never be the case in this family. A slight sniffle, then she lifted her chin, gaze steady once more. "It's good to be proven wrong."

"Speaking of wrong," Jamie said, "where's your other half in his wrong, ugly sweater?" From his suitcase that afternoon, Angel had produced a truly hideous silver and black Raiders and Reindeer ugly sweater that had gotten him good-naturedly razzed by everyone at the party.

"On the patio trying to flirt with one of the redheads. Talking cars to him, and all he does is talk back about baby goats. He a Talley too?"

"Nope, that's David. He belongs to the cowboy"—he pointed at Marsh in his snow-white Stetson—"and his husband, Levi, the blond beside him." They were chatting with Cam next to one of the TVs that had the football game on, Angel's team playing. "They're both FBI agents too."

"But David has red hair? How am I supposed to keep this all straight?"

"And the redheaded Madigans aren't even here yet."

She hung her head back on a dramatic sigh, a mannerism of Aidan's she'd already picked up.

"I'll draw you a diagram," Jamie said, before leaning closer to add, "And pro tip, hardly anyone in this family is straight."

"My kind of people," she said with a fist held out for a bump. Jamie bumped back, and when she surveyed the room again, he was glad to see it was with more curiosity than awe and trepidation. She gestured to where Katie, who she'd met earlier, stood chatting with Nic. "Who's that Katie is talking to?"

"Aidan's other best friend, Nic. Katie's favorite uncle, though don't tell Aidan."

"The long-suffering sports fan one?"

"Yeah, that's him."

"Okay, here goes nothing." She pushed off the couch, summoning up the confidence he and Aidan had recognized in her from day one, remarkable for someone who'd been through as much as she had at such a young age. She stepped to Katie's side, hand out to Nic. It didn't take but a minute for the group to laugh at something she said, and a minute after that, she had her head together with the two, plotting who knew what.

Jamie didn't get long to ponder before Aidan's mother, Ellen, lowered herself onto the couch beside him. "Hi, sweetie," she said, laying her free hand over his, the other holding the delicate stem of her champagne glass.

He leaned over, kissing her cheek. "Mom. Happy holidays."

"It is, isn't it?" she said. Her gaze made a lap of the room, all of her family gathered and in good spirits, before it landed back on him. "Thank you."

"For?"

"Making him happy." She nodded to where Aidan stood with Izzy, Mel, and Danny, laughing over what sounded like one of Izzy's in-flight stories. "I've missed that sight."

"He missed her too."

"And I heard Mel offered her a job."

Aidan had told him about Angel's idea, a great one, and he'd encouraged Aidan to talk to Mel about it. "Did you hear whether she accepted it?"

She tipped her champagne glass toward Danny. "My baby boy knows how to close a deal." Jamie chuckled. She spoke the truth, and he prayed Danny delivered on this one too. "I have a good feeling about it."

As she sipped her drink, Jamie's gaze flitted back to Nic, Katie, and Bev, who were crossing the room to join Aidan's group. Bev scooted around so she was next to Aidan, bumping his side. He lifted a hand, waited for her nod, and, when she gave it, wrapped it around her shoulders. She looped hers around his waist, leaning into him.

"I always knew he'd make a good father," Ellen said, and when Jamie glanced her way, he wasn't surprised to see tears in the corners of her eyes.

"I just hope I'll be half as good at it as him."

She squeezed his fingers, her grip as strong as he remembered from that night they'd first met, sitting on the porch together worried about Aidan. The worry was gone now, just happiness and certainty in her autumn eyes, the same color as Aidan's. "You'll be the best parents you can be," she assured him. "That's all any of us can do."

THIRTY-FIVE

One year later

Aidan woke much the same way as he had a little over a year ago—snuggled to his husband's side, an arm slung over his big, warm chest, Jamie's fingers gently carding through his hair. Only today they were in their own bed, in the downstairs primary of their San Francisco home, with the morning sun sneaking in around the edges of the patio door curtains.

With the pitter-patter of feet overhead.

He buried his smile in Jamie's side, the excess of love, of happiness too overwhelming sometimes. Even after a year of having Izzy and Angel back in their lives, a year of Bev in their lives too. Even after five months with all of them in San Francisco, five months with their daughter in their home.

Jamie continued to run his fingers through his hair, calming him. "Merry Christmas," he said once Aidan's breathing had returned to normal. His voice was still rough with sleep; he hadn't been awake long either.

Lifting his head, Aidan propped his chin on Jamie's chest. "Merry Christmas to you too." He kissed the tattoo over Jamie's heart, still a little red from where Jamie had recently added two dates to the design—their wedding date, and the date Bev's adoption had been finalized. Two dates that had irrevocably changed both their lives for the better.

A text ping sounded from Jamie's phone on the bedside table. He reached out a long arm and snagged it off the charger. "It's Izzy," he said. "She and Tag will be here in thirty." It had been love-at-first sight for Izzy and the other assistant coach who had recruited Jamie. She and Tag had married in October and lived not too far away. Close enough that Angel was able to pick Bev up for school every day in the truck that he, Jamie, and Celia—and Tag too— had spent months bringing back to life. "We need them to bring anything?"

Pots and pans clattered overhead.

"Backup breakfast," Aidan suggested.

Chuckling, Jamie tossed the phone back on the stand and swatted his ass. "The kids wanted to do something nice for us for Christmas morning. And you agreed to it."

"Yeah, after three of Jax's Manhattans last night at the party."

Jamie gave him another swat. "We have to trust them."

Aidan wasn't so sure they wouldn't be cooking second breakfast, but Jamie was right. He'd agreed to this deal and had to live with it. How bad could it turn out?

As if on cue, more clattering echoed from the kitchen upstairs. Aidan buried his face in Jamie's side again, muffling his laughter. Jamie's lips tickled his ear. "I couldn't sleep last night," he whispered. "So I got up and prepped a quiche. It's in the garage fridge, ready to be baked."

Aidan grinned up at him. "Will you marry me?"

He flitted his fingers, the emeralds of his wedding ring sparkling in the morning light. "Already did."

Aidan laced their fingers together, the aquamarine stones in his band likewise sparkling, almost as bright as Jamie's eyes. "I'd do it all over again to wind up right here with you. With the family I always wanted."

"Jesus, Irish." Jamie hauled him up, crashing their lips together and rolling Aidan onto his back. "The things you say to me."

Aidan planted a foot in the bed, knee propped between Jamie's thighs, nudging the backside of his balls, forcing Jamie to rock forward, bringing their stiffening cocks together. "The things you do to me."

Jamie trailed a line of kisses from his ear, along his jaw, down to the hollow of his throat. "How long do you think we have?"

"Twenty minutes, *max*, before they set off the fire alarm."

"I want to suck you off."

"Not enough time. I want inside you."

Jamie muffled his groan against Aidan's pec and rutted against him. Taking that as a yes, Aidan rolled Jamie back under him and slid a hand down his husband's chest and inside his boxers. Taking him in hand, he stroked his cock, once, twice, then ventured lower, teasing his taint.

Tapped his rim.

Jamie's back flew off the bed, bowing. "Fuck, Irish," he gutted out, voice low. "Quit teasing."

"Maybe I'll just tease you. Leave it at that."

Jamie shot a hand down, inside Aidan's boxers, fingers wrapping around his cock. "Two can play at that game."

A game Aidan would lose given how turned on he was already. In which case, he might as well lose—or rather, win—the way he really wanted to. "Get the lube," he said.

As Jamie stretched for the drawer, Aidan wriggled out of his boxers, then rid Jamie of his. He held out his hand, and Jamie squirted a generous amount into his palm and along his two extended fingers, their routine practiced now but no less hot for its efficiency.

How could it not be hot?

Readying himself under Jamie's heated stare, his pulse racing and cock swelling in anticipation.

Sinking his fingers inside his husband, the warmth and heat closing around him, drawing him in farther.

Finding the spot inside him that made Jamie's limbs tremble from pleasure overload, that made him bite his bottom lip to hold back the groans that rumbled deep in his chest.

Giving in to Jamie's whimpers and pleas to get inside him, never able to resist him for long.

Aidan thrust his cock inside his husband's ass and fell forward, hands braced on the mattress on either side of Jamie's head. He lifted his hips, drawing back to just the tip, then tunneled forward again, pegging Jamie's already sensitive prostate.

Jamie's mouth fell open, and Aidan swallowed his needy moans. Drowned in them as he claimed Jamie's mouth, kissing him deep and thorough, tongue sweeping every corner before tangling with Jamie's.

"Quiet, baby," he coached the coach, as he continued to drive harder and faster, pushing them closer to the edge.

He lowered onto an elbow, freeing his other hand to frame Jamie's cheek, to hold him in place as he lowered his mouth to Jamie's other ear. "This is the best Christmas morning of my life, Whiskey," he whispered there. "No matter how burnt those pancakes will be. No matter how many hours I spend today watching the wrong teams play. No matter how ugly the sweater is that I'll have to wear. It's fucking perfect, all of it, and you made it that way, Jamie. I wouldn't have any of this without you."

He drew back, finding Jamie's eyes open and wet, burning bright with the same love that scorched through Aidan. "Thank you for trusting me with this life. With this." He laid a hand over Aidan's heart. "I'll protect it with everything I am. Always."

He hitched his legs higher, holding Aidan deep as he threw them the rest of the way over the edge, coming with their mouths and bodies joined.

Their lives and hearts full.

"Always," Aidan echoed against his husband's lips, the same promise they'd made on their wedding day, the promise that would carry them into their future together.

———

Reviews are an invaluable tool when it comes to spreading the word about great reads. Please consider leaving an honest review for *Angel's Share* on your favorite review site.

Thank you for reading!

ACKNOWLEDGMENTS

When I finished writing *Agents Irish and Whiskey* the first time, back in 2018, I really didn't intend to come back to them. But as Aidan and Jamie continued to sneak into other stories, and as readers continued to ask how they were doing, I began to wonder the same myself.

Then, as I prepared the original books for re-release last year, I realized there were some loose ends that needed tying up. Being able to do that while also giving Aidan and Jamie an even happier ever after was a real treat. And none of it would've been possible without all the readers who have kept Irish and Whiskey in their hearts and on their reading lists over the years. I hope this story put as big a smile on your face as it did on mine. Thank you for cheering me and Aidan and Jamie on!

Big thanks as well to everyone on the team who contributed to this effort:

Christian Leatherman for narrating the audio for this book and for the AIW re-releases. You have been an absolute joy to work with, and thank you again for taking a chance on me, *What We May Be*, and that *Silent Knight* scene I threw at you years ago.

Kim on beta, Adam on edits, Lori on proofreading, and Becca and Theresa on marketing.

Cate coming in hot with the pink that perfectly set the

LA tone and made Wander's stunning photo of Matheus R. really pop.

Susie Selva on the Whiskey Verse timeline that made this book possible. No lie, I had it open the entire time. And shout out to Debra Akins for getting it into Airtable for me.

Jen and Megan at Grey's Promotions—y'all are the best—and all the ARC readers for getting the word out about the release.

Hailey and Annabeth for their tireless sprint partner devotion, and Allison and Erin for all the pep talks.

And finally a special shout-out to my own partner, Mr. Reyne, who had to deal with A LOT on this one. Life conspired to make my time super short to wrap this book up, and he stepped up big time with the cheers and the kitchen magic to power me across the finish line.

ALSO BY LAYLA REYNE

For the most up-to-date list of titles and a helpful reading order, please visit www.laylareyne.com.

Agents Irish and Whiskey:

Single Malt

Cask Strength

Barrel Proof

Tequila Sunrise

Blended Whiskey

Angel's Share

Fog City:

Prince of Killers

King Slayer

A New Empire

Queen's Ransom

Silent Knight

Perfect Play:

Dead Draw

Bad Bishop

King Hunt

Best Play

Standalone Stories:

What We May Be

Under the Table

Table for Two:

The Last Drop

Blue Plate Special

Over a Barrel

Changing Lanes:

Relay

Medley

Freestyle

Soul to Find:

Icarus and the Devil

Jason and the Storm

Paris and the Reaper

ABOUT THE AUTHOR

Layla Reyne is the author of *What We May Be* and the *Agents Irish and Whiskey, Fog City,* and *Perfect Play* series. She writes sexy, intense LGBTQIA+ romance featuring competent adults in kitchens, sports arenas, car chases, and other high-stakes situations. Whether it's adrenaline-fueled suspense, rival athletes, vampires and shifters in alt-realms, or love mixed with mouth-watering foodie goodness, queer folks finding happily-ever-afters is guaranteed.

You can find Layla at laylareyne.com, in her reader group on Facebook—Layla's Lushes, and at the following sites:

BB bookbub.com/authors/layla-reyne

f facebook.com/laylareyne

instagram.com/laylareyne

tiktok.com/@laylareyne

www.ingramcontent.com/pod-product-compliance
Lightning Source LLC
Chambersburg PA
CBHW060444310726
48977CB00001B/319